LEGISLATIVE ORIGINS OF THE NATIONAL AERONAUTICS AND SPACE ACT OF 1958

Proceedings of an Oral History Workshop

Conducted April 3, 1992

Moderated by John M. Logsdon

MONOGRAPHS IN AEROSPACE HISTORY

Number 8

National Aeronautics and Space Administration
NASA History Office
Office of Policy and Plans
Washington, DC 1998

For sale by the U.S. Government Printing Office
Superintendent of Documents, Mail Stop: SSOP, Washington, DC 20402-9328
ISBN: 978-1-78039-316-2

Contents

Foreword

In retrospect, it appears that the Soviet launch of *Sputniks 1* and *2* in the autumn of 1957 took place at exactly the right time to inspire the U.S. entrance into the space age. The ingredients were in place to begin space exploration already, but the Sputnik crisis prompted important legislation that brought many of these elements together into a single organization. By striking a blow at U.S. prestige, the Sputnik crisis had the effect of unifying groups that had been working separately on space missions, national defense, arms control, and within national and international organizations. The National Aeronautics and Space Act of 1958 was a tangible result of that national unification and accomplished one fundamental objective: it ensured that outer space would be a dependable, orderly place for beneficial pursuits.

There have been many detailed historical studies of the process of crafting and passing the the legislation that created the National Aeronautics and Space Administration (NASA). Signed into law by president Dwight D. Eisenhower on July 29, 1958, the "Space Act," as it came to be called, set forth a broad mission for NASA to "plan, direct, and conduct aeronautical and space activities"; to involve the nation's scientific community in these activities; and to disseminate widely information about these activities. The Act remains the core statement governing United States civil space exploration activities, launching as it did an organization that preempted outer space for peaceful exploration and uses that Americans have now enjoyed for forty years.

At the time of the fortieth anniversary of NASA, it seems appropriate to revisit the origins of the Space Act. Consequently, the NASA History Office chose to publish a monograph containing the recollections of key participants in the legislative process. The collective oral history presented here originated in 1992 and included the following participants:

- **Paul G. Dembling** was the general counsel of the National Advisory Committee for Aeronautics (NACA) during the critical 1957–1958 period and played a principal role in drafting the bill which ultimately became the National Aeronautics and Space Act of 1958. He later served as the NASA general counsel.

- **Eilene Galloway** served as Senior Specialist in International Relations (National Security) for the Congressional Research Service. Following the launching of Sputnik 1, she was Special Consultant to Senator Lyndon B. Johnson and to Representative John W. McCormack during congressional hearings on the "Space Act."

- **George E. Reedy** was the senior advisor to Senator Lyndon B. Johnson, Senate Majority Leader, in 1957 and 1958 during the Sputnik crisis and the consideration of legislation that eventually became the "Space Act."

- **Gerald W. Siegel** served during the 1950s in various staff positions with the Senate, including those of counsel to the Democratic Policy Committee and the preparedness investigating subcommittee of the Senate Armed Services Committee. He also served de facto as staff director of the Senate Special Committee on Space and Aeronautics during 1958 when it considered the "Space Act."

- **Willis H. Shapley** was a member of the Bureau of the Budget during 1957–1958, where he eventually became director for space program coordination. In 1965 he moved to NASA as associate deputy administrator, with his duties including supervision of the public affairs, congressional affairs, interagency affairs, and international affairs offices.

- **H. Guyford Stever** was on the faculty at the Massachusetts Institute of Technology during the Sputnik crisis and during the creation of NASA in 1957–1958. He became directly involved in the "Space Act" as a member of the Air Force scientific advisory board. He also served in a number of other science policy capacities with the National Research Council and the National Science Foundation, as well as science advisor to President Gerald Ford.

- **Glen P. Wilson** was a staff member for the Senate during the Sputnik crisis and participated in the writing of the National Aeronautics and Space Act of 1958 and later served on the Senate Committee on Aeronautical and Space Sciences throughout its entire existence from 1958 until the Senate reorganization in 1977.

The valuable perspective these individuals provide deepen and expand our understanding of this important historical event.

This gathering of participants was organized through the efforts of the Space Policy Institute at The George Washington University in Washington, D.C., and the Lyndon Baines Johnson Presidential Library in Austin, Texas.

This is the eighth in a series of special studies prepared by the NASA History Division. The **Monographs in Aerospace History** series is designed to provide a wide variety of investigations relative to the history of aeronautics and space. These publications are intended to be tightly focused in terms of subject, relatively short in length, and reproduced in an inexpensive format to allow timely and broad dissemination to researchers in aerospace history. Suggestions for additional publications in the **Monographs in Aerospace History** series are welcome.

ROGER D. LAUNIUS
Chief Historian
National Aeronautics and Space Administration
May 25, 1998

Preface and Acknowledgments

The idea for getting on the record the recollections of those who had worked on space issues in the U.S. Congress during the immediate post-Sputnik through the passage of the National Aeronautics and Space Act of 1958 came from Glen P. Wilson. Dr. Wilson, who in 1957 and 1958 was a junior staff member working for Lyndon B. Johnson, had been involved in the U.S. space program since its origins, and he convinced the Space Policy Institute at George Washington University and the Lyndon Baines Johnson Library that there was a story that had not been fully told about the role of the Congress, and particularly of Senator Lyndon B. Johnson and those that worked with him, in the process that resulted in setting up a new civilian space agency in 1958. The two organizations at Glen's urging decided to work together to bring together as many as possible of those who were involved in that process and to let them reminisce about their involvement in the events of 1957 and 1958.

These reminiscences took the form of a three-hour workshop that was recorded on videotape in the studios of GW Television on the campus of the George Washington University in downtown Washington, D.C., on April 3, 1992. This document and the videotape of the workshop itself are being made available to various archives and research centers concerned with space and with the major personalities of the time.

The workshop would not have been possible without the financial support of the Lyndon Baines Johnson Foundation and the personal involvement of the Director of the Johnson Library, Harry Middleton, and his associate, Robert Hardesty. Kimberly Carter, Executive Aide at the Space Policy Institute, managed the preparations for the workshop with skill and good cheer. Susan Brown and her crew at GW television added professionalism to the videotaped production. The ability of the Space Policy Institute to undertake worthwhile projects such as this is a result of the generosity of the several corporate contributors to the Institute's work.

Of course, all of us involved in organizing this workshop owe great thanks to our seven participants, both for sharing their experiences with us and for the contributions they have made to their country, both at the beginning of the Space Age and throughout their careers.

JOHN M. LOGSDON
Director
Space Policy Institute
George Washington University

Introduction

The October 4, 1957, launch by the Soviet Union of the first artificial Earth satellite, Sputnik 1, came as a shock to most in the United States. The fact that a Russian space launch was imminent was known to individuals at top levels of government and the scientific community, but little had been done to prepare for the public reaction to that event. That reaction clearly surprised President Dwight Eisenhower and his advisors. The reaction to Sputnik shocked the American political system into action. Within a year after Sputnik, a comprehensive National Aeronautics and Space Act of 1958 had been passed by Congress, and signed by the President. This created a new space agency, the National Aeronautics and Space Administration (NASA), and important elements of both the civilian and military space program had gotten a kick start.

Another of the impacts of Sputnik was to convince President Eisenhower that he needed direct access to the advice of the scientific community. To do so, he created the post of Science Advisor to the President, and he named James R. Killian, Jr., the President of the Massachusetts Institute of Technology (MIT), to that post. Many years later, Dr. Killian wrote about the creation of the National Aeronautics and Space Act.[1] He noted that many influences were brought to bear on the formulation of the legislation, as they

While President Dwight D. Eisenhower had shown an interest in space activities, especially for national defense objectives, prior to the launch of Sputnik 1 *on October 4, 1957, he failed to recognize the important psychological affect the launch of the Soviet satellite would have on the American people. Here he is shown in the Oval Office with the recovered nosecone from a Jupiter-C missile carried 1,200 miles downrange on August 7, 1957, before a national television audience. (NASA photograph)*

---

1. James R. Killian, Jr., *Sputnik, Scientists, and Eisenhower* (Cambridge, MA: MIT Press, 1977).

should have been. He observed that the final act represented a remarkable blending of the interests, needs, and objectives of the Administration, the Department of Defense, and the scientific community. Killian's observation was correct as far as it went, but it was not complete. There was another major actor in the process of giving shape to the U.S. space program: the U.S. Congress. While there is much on the public record regarding the debates within the Eisenhower Administration on how best to organize the U.S. space program, there has been relatively little attention paid to its legislative origins. That was the basic rationale for this workshop: to provide some perspective on the role that Congress played in creating an enduring and productive framework for America's activities in space.

Many in Congress took on key roles, but perhaps the single most influential individual was Senate Majority Leader Lyndon Baines Johnson. Senator Johnson was at his Texas ranch the night Sputnik was launched, and from that night until he addressed the United Nations on the need for cooperation in the peaceful uses of space, thirteen months later, LBJ was at the center of congressional debate over space. It is thus appropriate that the Johnson Library was a co-organizer of this event, and that several of Senator Johnson's close associates participated in the workshop. The format of the workshop was to begin with one-on-one discussions with each of the seven individuals who were able to be part of this workshop. Then all of the participants came together for a concluding roundtable. Each participant played an important role in the events of late 1957 and 1958. The goal of the workshop was to let them tell their part of the story as they remember it.

Thus the following pages are a transcript of the workshop discussions, edited for purposes of clarity and with addenda from the interviewees. The interviewer is John M. Logsdon. In preparation for the workshop, Glen Wilson prepared an extremely useful background paper on "How the U.S. Space Act Came to Be." That paper is included as an Appendix to these proceedings.

Individual Discussions

Conversation with George E. Reedy

Our first conversation is with **George E. Reedy,** *who has had a distinguished career as an educator, author, and public servant. Mr. Reedy was, of course, press secretary and consultant to Lyndon Johnson. He later became Dean of the College of Journalism at Marquette University. He is author of* The Twilight of the Presidency *and many other books and articles. During the 1950s, Mr. Reedy served on the staff of the Senate Preparedness Subcommittee and from 1955 to 1960 was Staff Director of the Democratic Policy Committee of the Congress, one of the many Congressional organizations that felt the strong influence of Lyndon Johnson.*

Logsdon: Mr. Reedy, thank you for joining us today.

Reedy: Good to be here.

Logsdon: Give us a sense of how you and Senator Johnson interacted on the space issue in the immediate aftermath of Sputnik and then as the space program took shape during 1958.

Reedy: Well, in the immediate aftermath, for about two weeks I merely let the thing vegetate. Senator Johnson had so many problems on his mind that I doubt whether he devoted too much attention to it. We were both down in Texas. I was living in Austin there at the time. We had some very difficult years ahead of us. The next year was going to be a campaign year, which meant that the Senate would be very difficult to lead and for a while I sort of put the space thing on the back burner. But what got me out of it was a visit from Charles S. Brewton, who has now unfortunately passed away, but for whose political acumen I had great deal of respect. I think that if there is a father to the Space Act it was probably Charley Brewton, of whom very few people have ever heard. Charley had been Senator Lister Hill's administrative assistant. I had never known him to be wrong in judging the public. He came down to see me, and said that the Space Act was so tremendous. It could first of all clobber the Republicans, secondly lead to tremendous advances, and, third, elect Lyndon Johnson as president. Well, I told him that Lyndon Johnson was not interested in running for the presidency. He said that was all right with him, he would settle for clobbering the Republicans. He was a Democrat. He insisted we drive out of Austin and out into the hill country right around Austin. We found a little mound where we could look and see hundreds of miles of practically nothing. He began to talk about the space program; that man had really mastered the drift of it, the poetry. He didn't know very much about outer space but he had grasped immediately the fact that this was something that could change the whole way that we lived; it could change our nation. He convinced me. I remember going back that night. My mind was just full of it. I sat up most of the night reading everything that I could. And I wrote the Senator a long memorandum the next day, which went beyond Charley's thinking because I knew a little more about space.

Logsdon: This was October 17?

Reedy: Right, October 17, 1957. I wrote a rather lengthy memorandum. In that memorandum, I said that this would go far beyond a mere defense thing. The immediate public reaction would probably be fear, but that long range, this could be one of the great dividing lines in American and world history, the whole history of humanity. I remember the Senator as being a little bit reluctant at first, because he had so many other problems on his mind and they were pressing him. Finally, we went to Washington, where we met with Senator Russell and I have a feeling Senator Bridges—my memory's not clear. We had a very private briefing, in the Pentagon, on the state of America's rocket program. As I remember, there were some rather amusing aspects to it. That is where we first learned about Atlas and Polaris and all of those things. It became apparent to us, at the time, that the Defense Department was thinking solely in military terms, which was not really what we were after. We thought that something more than that was in effect. So, at the end of the hearing, we went back to the Hill and met in Senator Russell's office. What Senator Russell did was to authorize Johnson to use the Senate Preparedness Subcommittee to hold some hearings into this whole question. That Subcommittee had been defunct for a number of years. It was appointed, originally, to look into events in Korea during the Korean War. We started gathering people that could be useful. Eventually this led to the first set of hearings at which Edwin Weisel in New York acted as a consultant counsel, and Cy Vance, who was out of Ed Weisel's law firm, also was an assistant consulting counsel. That brought Eilene Galloway into it and quite a number of other people.

Logsdon: These were the hearings in November–December 1957 that led to a set of recommendations in early January 1958?

Reedy: Right. Those were the hearings.

Logsdon: And then Senator Johnson went before the Democratic Policy Committee and spoke on the space issue?

Reedy: Right.

Logsdon: Were you directly involved with that?

Reedy: Only to the extent of distributing the speech. What had happened was that the speech was written by Horace Busby. It was a remarkable speech, sort of an overpowering speech.

Logsdon: In *Twilight of the Presidency* you call it a "compelling power."

Reedy: Right, which is a good way to describe it. One felt almost that one were listening to an Old Testament prophet. I think that was a very important influence in selling the space program. We were already running into some troubles, because it was apparent that President Eisenhower was very reluctant and so was the Pentagon to open this up to the civilian exploration program. They were thinking almost entirely in terms of weaponry. The weaponry was rather well developed. The one real advantage that the Russians had over us, at that point, was that they had developed rockets which were much more powerful than ours.

Logsdon: Because they had a heavier warhead?

No one understood the importance of the launch of Sputnik for the psyche of the American people more effectively than Senate Majority Leader Lyndon B. Johnson. Here he is shown as president on September 15, 1964, at a meeting hosted by NASA, the agency that he helped to create with the National Aeronautics and Space Act of 1958. (NASA photograph 64-H-2360)

Reedy: No, just because they started earlier. As nearly as we can make out what happened, the Russians, at some point, discovered that they could never catch up to us in powered aircraft. You know, once you get a momentum going.

Logsdon: Sure, and so they wanted to make a leap.

Reedy: They wanted to leapfrog and they leapfrogged to rocketry. If we were to get our rockets into space we had to put three rockets together to lift one small payload that the Russians could lift with one rocket. I think that to a great extent the Pentagon wanted to keep the thing as secret as they possibly could. They were also worried about the diversion of attention from weaponry into what they thought were nonproductive fields.

Logsdon: Space spectaculars.

Reedy: Right. I remember there were some remarks that leaked out of the White House. I think it was Sherman Adams, Eisenhower's top assistant, who made some remark about Lyndon Johnson playing outer space basketball. Eisenhower, at one point is supposed to have said, "Lyndon Johnson can keep his head in the stars if he wants. I'm going to keep my feet on the ground." There was very distinct reluctance for them to proceed, which, to me, raises a very interesting point. More than anything else, I'm a political theoretician and historian and this is one of the very few instances in this century, I can only think of three or four, where the initiative for a very major law and a very major change was the initiative of Congress.

Logsdon: Congress?

Reedy: Yes, Congress rather than the President.

Logsdon: Congress really put the pressure on the White House?

Reedy: Right.

Logsdon: I think the White House had to respond and brought a Space Act up, but it is because Congress was insistent.

Reedy: Right, and the Space Act was not a very good act that they brought up. Again, I think Eisenhower was afraid of having an agency that could get out of control. I don't think any of his motives, by the way, were bad or venal or anything like that. I think it was just a difference of opinion; and, therefore, he tried to keep the agency as much under control as possible and as much under the control of the military as he possibly could. You know, as a rule, if you take a look at a legislative year, the legislation consists of Congress reacting to what the President proposes.

Logsdon: Yes, to White House initiatives.

Reedy: Which doesn't mean the President gets everything he wants, not by a long shot. But, he has the power of the initiative. That's the one real power of the Presidency, by the way. There are not many others.

Logsdon: It is agenda setting.

Reedy: Right. Most of the powers of the Presidency are mythical, as every President has discovered. But here you had one of the only three or four instances I can think of in this century where something originated with Congress.

Logsdon: How engaged did Senator Johnson stay with the space issue after these early months in 1958. Was it a continuing concern? Of course, he had lots of other things on his mind.

Reedy: Right. It was a continuing concern, to a point. One of the problems here is it was an unusually difficult year. You have to realize that we were engaged in an election year. And the Senate and the House are always more difficult to manage. The Senate is a little bit easier than the House because only one third of the Senate is up in any particular election. There were many other things during that year. We also had a mild recession that came later in the year that meant that we had to do something about the economy, jump starting it, that sort of thing. I think for a while, Lyndon Johnson didn't get distracted from the space program, but he had many other things competing with it.

Logsdon: But, then, later in the year, and I believe you were involved, Senator Johnson was asked by President Eisenhower to go up to the United Nations and talk about the international aspects of the space program.

Reedy: Right, which was very fitting. You know, it was rather strange. If one looks at the press of the period, it became apparent immediately that Lyndon Johnson was the major innovator in this whole thing. I can still remember one marvelous cartoon that appeared in the Baltimore *Sun* showing Lyndon Johnson and the rest arriving like visitors from Mars. You know, "Take me to your leader," that kind of stuff, meaning the space program. He was the ideal man to make that statement before the United Nations, because you could really say that he was speaking for the country. He had originated this; it had been accepted by the nation; so he was the presenter.

Logsdon: Well, there's lots more I guess we could say, but we've run out of time for today. We'll get a chance when we all come back together. And thank you very much.

Conversation with Willis H. Shapley

Willis Shapley *is the prototype of the anonymous but remarkably effective and influential civil servant. Willis came to Washington in 1942 from his graduate studies at the University of Chicago for what he thought was a brief wartime tour of duty in the Bureau of the Budget. But he has never left Washington. He stayed with the Bureau of the Budget for twenty-three years, specializing in defense issues, and, after 1957, the space program. Then he became a senior staff advisor to NASA's Administrators from 1965 to 1975 and was called back from retirement after the* Challenger *accident to help stabilize NASA and the space program. In the post-Sputnik White House, the Bureau of the Budget had an important role in shaping the Administration's proposals for how to organize the nation's space effort, and Willis Shapley was in the midst of those discussions.*

Logsdon: Thank you for joining us today, Willis. What was your role in that immediate post-Sputnik period in thinking through how to respond to what the nation needed in space?

Shapley: Well, I and my colleagues were a part of the Executive Office of the President and so setting policy direction and deciding political reactions were really beyond our scope. Of course, we all had personal ideas of one sort or another but as the Administration position, as the record shows, changed gradually over the period that we're talking

Willis Shapley had been a member of the Bureau of the Budget during 1957–1958, where he eventually became director for space program coordination. In 1965, he moved to NASA as associate deputy administrator, with his duties including supervision of the public affairs, congressional affairs, interagency affairs, and international affairs offices. He is shown here being sworn in to his NASA position by Administrator James E. Webb. (NASA photograph)

about, our role was mainly to help steer it in what seemed to be the right direction, and to find ways of dealing with the substantive policy matters that needed to be addressed.

Logsdon: Well, talk about the kind of changing forces in guidance that you people were getting from the political leadership.

Shapley: I think I should first say that there were a couple of things in the background that influenced things a lot more than, or at least as much as what was happening in space. A few years before Sputnik, perhaps about a year and a half, the President had approved giving the ballistic missile programs top national priority. That was taken very seriously. The highest national priority started out being given to the Atlas missile, the Titan, and later the Polaris when it came along.

Logsdon: Thor and Jupiter were in there, too.

Shapley: My job in the Bureau of the Budget, as you mentioned, was in what was called the military division at that time. We had a way of working jointly with the Department of Defense. We actually served *de facto* as staff under the Secretary of Defense as well as staff for the Director of the Bureau of the Budget. These were two separate roles which we played. In the case of ballistic missiles, the decision was made to set up what was called a red-line organization—the Ballistic Missile Committee—to get all the bureaucracy out of the way and to have the principal officials meet once a week or every ten days to make the decisions right in the room to keep the programs going. The Bureau of the Budget was one member of that. I was the alternate to the Assistant Director who was our member, which meant that I was in the midst of it. Our policies at the time were not a matter of emphasis on military as against civilian as far as space was concerned; it was firmly believed and directed by the President that the ballistic missile programs should be top priority. As you may recall, he had been somewhat pushed into that position earlier, but now this was a very real concern. And so, in the early days of Vanguard, anything to be done about space was going to have to be done without interfering with the ballistic missile program.

Logsdon: But clearly Sputnik changed the calculus a little?

Shapley: The system reacted very promptly to Sputnik. I think it was less than a month after Sputnik or even less than that; perhaps it was after *Sputnik 2*. The ballistic missile committee and the Secretary of Defense ordered von Braun's people to go ahead with a satellite. A few weeks later, the decision was made to establish ARPA as a whole new agency in the Department of Defense, something that would have been unthinkable without Sputnik because it cut across all the services.

Logsdon: When ARPA was set up, was there a thought that that might be the space agency?

Shapley: I don't think the idea of a need for a space agency or that there would be one had permeated enough people's thinking at that time. ARPA was something that needed to be done. It was the quickest way of doing it. The wonderful thing about business in those days was this could be done. It was effectively done even before the various congressional catch-up things were done. And, of course, nobody was against doing it. They got people right away. Roy Johnson was the first Director, I believe. It went to work. We very carefully designed the language setting it up so that it wouldn't necessarily be a permanent bureaucracy; it could take money from the services and transfer it somewhere else; it could take its own money and give it to the services.

Logsdon: It was the place that the space program was at least temporarily placed in early 1958.

Shapley: That's right. Certainly space and, incidentally, anti-missile programs were put there, too, which shows that the focus wasn't entirely space. Now the other main thing in the background, I think, is that during this period there were successive waves of unification in the Department of Defense and it is hard to believe, from the way things are now, how vigorous, dirty even, the interservice fighting in the Department of Defense was and how every step to increase the authority of the Secretary of Defense over the Departments in any way ran into all sorts of resistance, end runs to Congress, and everything. And this is another matter in which we in the Bureau of the Budget were very much involved: helping strengthen the Department of Defense. There were successive reorganizations of the R&D function in the Office of the Secretary of Defense, establishment of the Special Assistant for Guided Missiles, William M. Holaday, and other things of that sort.

Logsdon: So in the middle of this comes the space issue and the need to respond.

Shapley: Right. The point I'd like to emphasize is that the President, assisted by the Bureau of the Budget, the Secretary of Defense, and others were really all on the same side throughout this whole exercise of the response to Sputnik. There were really no policy differences. People over in the Pentagon were relying on us to help them make the decisions they made, and on the question of whether it should be a civilian agency or not. It was clear that there was going to be an agency; this was maybe in November. There was not the slightest doubt anywhere that it would be a civilian agency among the people that were controlling things. Now, the Air Force had a slightly different idea. The record shows that in November, General Putt in the Air Force set up a whole Directorate of Astronautics. Three days later, Secretary McElroy abolished it. Although there may have been other considerations, that was a symptom of what the Air Force expectations were. The Secretary of Defense wanted to prevent any of the services, especially the Air Force, from running away on its own on getting this new issue or any other issue. I think this background is very much part of the whole picture.

Logsdon: Well, the final recommendation to President Eisenhower that a new civilian agency based on the National Advisory Committee on Aeronautics came in the form of a March 5, 1958, memorandum. It came from the Advisory Committee on Government Organization, Nelson Rockefeller's group; but, it also came from BOB and the new President's Science Advisor. What's some of the background of that recommendation?

Shapley: Well, I have to confess that until somebody told me about that recommendation in preparing for this workshop, I had not really remembered it. I guess it was a significant external event that reflected basic decisions that had been made several weeks and months before that. The formal status, as I recall, was that the President appointed Mr. Killian to be his Science Advisor; Mr. Killian had a Space Subcommittee.

Logsdon: Ed Purcell headed the Space Subcommittee?

Shapley: Yes, Ed Purcell, and many other people. We in the Bureau of the Budget sat in with them on many of their meetings. When they turned to organization, we briefed them on our views—more on that in a moment—and explained what the pros and cons were. And so

This was the official seal for the National Advisory Committee for Aeronautics (NACA), which was established by act of Congress in March 1915. The seal depicts the first flight of the Wright brothers in December 1903. The NACA made up the core of the new National Aeronautics and Space Administration. (NASA photograph 90-H-537)

by the time the memorandum was written and signed, the whole thing was really sort of a done deal. Although I'm not sure everybody knew it was a done deal, it certainly was.

Logsdon: All right. You wanted to talk a bit about what the Bureau of the Budget brought to this discussion.

Shapley: In the Bureau of the Budget at that time, besides the responsibilities for budgets, organization, and programs in the individual agencies, it also had the responsibility for seeking to preserve the integrity of organization of the government as a whole. In those days, there was a standing piece of legislation that was renewed each year called the Reorganization Act, which gave the President broad authority to reorganize the government, subject only to congressional veto. There was a very high caliber professional group in the Bureau called the Government Organization Branch, and whenever there was going to be any reorganization proposed or considered they were the professionals that dealt with it. At this time, the head of that whole Division was William F. Finan. He assigned as Project Officer Alan Dean, who was the staff person involved. From the other side of the Bureau of the Budget, where I was, in effect, the chief person involved in space matters, we assigned one or two people. Wreatham Gathright and, I think, one other sat with the group. You are going to have other members of the group on the program here a little bit later. Their job was to actually draft a bill and that is what they did.

Logsdon: Now, that bill was sent to the Congress in April and then both the Senate and House had hearings and proposed a bunch of changes. How vigorously were those changes resisted at the Executive end?

Shapley: Virtually, not at all, as far as I recall, although I should say that I was not directly involved in the relations with Congress during this period.

Logsdon: That would have been Bryce Harlow's office.

Shapley: Normally a bill drafted in the Bureau of the Budget would be defended by the people who were going to implement it. In this case that was Dr. Dryden from NACA, and other witnesses. The heart of the bill that I was concerned with, beside just the technicalities and formalities you need for a new agency, was the question of the role of the Department of Defense. People were for a civilian agency, for all sorts of reasons. In some parts of the arena, there were people who denied or greatly underestimated the importance, long-run, of space to the Department of Defense. This was something which I can truthfully say, I had some slight glimmer of, although at that time no great conviction. And so the way the bill was drafted, the language prepared, which was in the original Administration bill and remained in the final one said that space activities will be under a civilian agency except for activities primarily related to the Department of Defense. Well, what happened in the Congress, basically, was that the bill spelled out the role of the Department of Defense in much greater detail. Now, this was not something that the Administration resisted, except on a sort of vague ground of principle. They regretted it, because one of the guiding lights in writing reorganizations from the Executive Branch standpoint, is to leave everybody flexibility. I think it can be said that all the changes that were made in the bill, most of which were in my opinion improvements or clarifications, authorized things that could have been done anyway. They were covered by authorities that the agencies already had. I think the Defense Department could have done everything authorized in the final Act under the Administration bill (except maybe setting up that military liaison committee which turned out not to be a very useful thing and was dropped).

Logsdon: Through this whole process, and, in particular, when the Administration was considering the bill and a new agency, Congress, particularly Preparedness Investigating Subcommittee, was conducting hearings? Was there an interaction? Was there much influence on the part of the Congress, or were you operating pretty much within the Executive Branch?

Shapley: Well I was. I'm sure people were reading the hearings as a standard procedure and others in the Bureau were working with Congress. But basically, I think, there was a certain amount of executive arrogance, if you please. We saw organization as our business and felt we knew how to organize agencies just as well as anybody else; while they also felt they understood the problem as far as setting up a new agency was concerned. But all this is completely separate, really, from the questions of how emotional you get about space, how important space was, how big a deal. I think the Administration clearly underestimated the public impact of space. On the other hand, the bill as it came out has stood up pretty well. So maybe the work on the bill was not all bad.

Logsdon: Right. Thank you very much for being with us today.

Shapley: Thank you.

Conversation with Gerald W. Siegel

*Our next guest, **Gerald Siegel** is a lawyer by training. During the 1950s he served in various staff positions in the Senate, including counsel to the Democratic Policy Committee and the Preparedness Investigating Subcommittee. He was the de facto staff director of the Senate Special Committee on Space and Astronautics as it considered the Administration's proposal for a Space Act during the first half of 1958. Mr. Siegel left the Senate shortly thereafter to lecture for three years at Harvard and then served as the Vice President and Chief Counsel of the Washington Post until his retirement.*

Logsdon: Glad you could be with us today, Mr. Siegel. I understand that on the night that Sputnik went up, October 4, 1957, you were at the Johnson ranch working with the Senator. What kind of reaction did he have?

Siegel: It was a very interesting reaction. My wife and I had gone to Austin to explore the possibility of moving to Texas to work for Mrs. Johnson and her television station. I had told the Senator a year before that I was going to leave the staff, and so, when we got the news, probably by telephone, as he frequently did when he had things that he wanted to mull over, he said, "let's take a walk to Cousin Oriole's." Cousin Oriole was a legitimate cousin, who lived on the ranch about five hundred yards or so away in a small house, and was an unlettered but very wise woman who frequently was the environment provider for much of the cerebration that he would undertake. So we went down there and talked. He thought through what he wanted to do. I think, unlike what George Reedy's recollection is, that at this time, the space program was not born in anybody's mind, that I'm aware of, who was dealing with what we then did. The Senator decided to call Senator Russell and Senator Bridges, that night.

Logsdon: Right, both were on the Armed Services Committee.

Siegel: And Johnson got approval to launch an investigation by the Preparedness Subcommittee into the missile and satellite program.

Logsdon: Right. The night of Sputnik.

Siegel: The very night of Sputnik. Either that night or, perhaps, the next day we called Solis Horowitz, one of the lawyers in Washington with our group, and had him begin to set up appointments for briefings for us. These ultimately came about. I went back to Washington probably on the 5th or 6th of October and stayed there. At that time the Senator was back and forth.

Logsdon: But the context was a security fear?

Siegel: I think that, one, there was fear because of this sudden demonstration of Russian technical expertise in a field where we didn't anticipate it, and, two, the military implications of it were foremost in our minds. I remember one of us saying, it wasn't the satellite we were concerned about, it was what got it up there.

Logsdon: The rocket.

Siegel: Because if you can achieve a missile launch of that magnitude, you can launch a thermonuclear bomb very easily.

Logsdon: Indeed.

Siegel: This was what was foremost. In a very short time the Administration, I think, probably ahead of even Charley Brewton who had the task of persuading George, who, in turn, was very influential with the Senator, everybody began to reflect upon, to the best of their ability, with limited if any knowledge, what a space program might consist of. We drafted no bills. There were Senators who did and dropped some in the hopper in the Senate. We waited. I don't recall if there was much interchange during the period in January and February and even into March between the Senator and the White House. If there was any, he had put me together with Bryce Harlow during the missile and satellite investigation. Bryce was our contact on such troublesome issues as the Gaither Report, which was disclosed and wasn't supposed to be.

Logsdon: That's right. Which was a report that said American bases were vulnerable to Soviet attack.

Siegel: Right. Some people wanted to believe it and some people didn't.

Logsdon: Talk a bit about the Preparedness Subcommittee hearings.

Siegel: Well, that subcommittee, as George Reedy indicated, was born in 1950 when Korea broke out and it did a large number of widespread studies that were issued in the form of reports, all unanimous, and all contributing, I think, to the election of Dwight Eisenhower. The Democrats really weren't very happy with it. The Subcommittee did stay in existence actually somewhere into 1956 or 1957, but it had dropped its activity considerably, but it had conducted the MacArthur Hearings. There was a slight fracas that came in 1951 when George came aboard. It did a number of important studies in the missile field in those early years.

Logsdon: In this immediate aftermath of Sputnik in November and December there were intense hearings with lots and lots of witnesses called.

Siegel: Well, the November/December/January hearings were indeed intense and they involved some of the best scientific minds in the country, experts in the military who had been on missile programs for military purposes.

Logsdon: So, the central thrust of those hearings really was what did this mean for U.S. security.

Siegel: There was one question: why did the Russians beat us with [our effort on] this little Geophysical Year Navy project that was supposed to launch an eleven pound satellite?

Logsdon: This was the Navy's Vanguard project. The Senate formed a Special Committee on Space and Astronautics, I think in anticipation of what the Administration was going to do.

Siegel: Oh, I think one of the recommendations by the time the missile and satellite investigation ended was that we had to do something about a space exploration program. What we were going to do was not well formulated at this point, but it was Senator Johnson's idea that there had to be a Blue Ribbon Committee and, indeed, it was a Blue Ribbon Committee.

The official American entrant into the scientific satellite effort undertaken as a result of the International Geophysical Year (IGY) in 1957-1958 was Project Vanguard. As an attempt to demonstrate parity with the Soviet Sputnik success, on December 6, 1957, the United States attempted to launch a Vanguard satellite, with spectacular lack of success. A malfunction in the first stage caused the vehicle to explode two seconds after launch. This failure gave added impetus to the legislative effort to create a separate agency dedicated to space exploration. (NASA photograph 67-H-1563)

Logsdon: Talk a little bit about the composition of the membership.

Siegel: The members were the Chairman and ranking members of the committees having some jurisdiction in the vague area of space exploration: Appropriations, Foreign Relations, Armed Services, Commerce.

Logsdon: Senator Johnson was the Chair of the Committee. What was the Committee doing before the Administration bill came up?

Siegel: The Special Committee?

Logsdon: Yes. Was it just getting itself organized and ready?

Siegel: I'll tell you my recollection, that is that Senator Johnson and Senator Bridges spent some time interviewing for a Counsel for the Committee. After talking with several people Senator Bridges suggested to Senator Johnson that they should save money and just let Gerry run it. And that's just what they decided to do. We never hired a Counsel.

Logsdon: The Administration bill came up in April; you had already laid a pretty firm foundation with the Preparedness Hearings, so you had, I think, four or five days of hearings on the bill.

Siegel: Most of us had never seen or heard about it and I think the Senator's characterization of it was that it was a bill formulated on a motorcycle going through the Pentagon.

Logsdon: So the reception of the Administration's bill wasn't too positive?

Siegel: At first it was not, but I think that ultimately it was determined that the basic substantive provisions of the Administration bill, and what the Senate Committee would want to see in such a bill, were not too different. Eilene Galloway did some early analysis of the bill and it began to emerge that there were some aspects of it that were not to the liking of the members of the Committee, or for the most part, perhaps, Senator Johnson, the Chairman. This was frequently a one or two man kind of operation. What I am drawing upon comes from a symposium that was held in September of 1959 by the American Political Science Association, with Bill Finan, who Willis Shapley mentioned, as the principal speaker. I spoke, along with a number of other people, of our recollections which were a good deal sharper than mine today about the organization of the program for space exploration in this country.

Logsdon: Is this something you wanted to read for our record?

Siegel: I would just try to summarize briefly, [our concerns included]: The lack of a specifically designated authority having major policy responsibility for the overall national space program, which is the birth of the Space Council. The ambiguity of the language in Section II of the proposed bill in which it was intended to set forth the respective jurisdictions of the Pentagon and the civilian agency, always fuzzy, always worrisome. Although, and I might mention, from what I have read, President Eisenhower was really only interested in the military aspects in the early stages. The absence of specific and appropriately qualified authority for international cooperation was not taken care of in the bill. The absence of any provisions relating to property rights and inventions, patent provisions, had to come. The House took the leadership. I worked with the staff person over there all the time, and we didn't put it in the Senate bill, we left it to be worked out in conference. We proposed to give the new space agency salaries equivalent to those in private industry. You see, even thirty-four years ago, we worried about compensation of executives.

Logsdon: Talk a little bit about the relations between the Senate and the House Committees as the Congress tried to agree on its view on a Space Act.

Siegel: The only thing I recall is that the thrust of the House approach began to point toward an agency headed by a commission as against an administrator.

Logsdon: A single headed agency? The Senate and Executive Branch preferred the Administration's bill?

Siegel: We worked that out by dropping the likeness to the Atomic Energy Commission.

Logsdon: Ultimately Senator Johnson went to see President Eisenhower and they reached some areas of compromise, so that there could be an agreed upon bill. Can you give us any insight?

Siegel: He didn't tell me he was going; or, if he did, I've forgotten it, because I didn't go.

Logsdon: Okay, so this was a one-on-one meeting?

Siegel: You know as much about it as I do.

Logsdon: Thank you for sharing your memories with us this afternoon.

Siegel: Happy to do it.

Conversation with Glen P. Wilson

Glen P. Wilson is, first of all, probably the primary moving spirit behind today's event. Glen convinced us that there was an important and untold story about Congressional influence in the early days of the U.S. space program. I think that what we've already heard today validates Glen's point. Glen Wilson has his doctorate in psychology. He came to Washington in 1955 to work for Lyndon Johnson. In 1957 in the wake of Sputnik, Glen was assigned by LBJ to the staff of the Preparedness Investigating Subcommittee. When the Senate established a Special Committee on Space and Astronautics, in early 1958, Glen became one of its initial staff members. It was that Committee, of course, that considered the Administration's proposal for a new space agency. When a standing Committee on Space was established by the Senate later in 1959, Glen joined its staff and served until the Committee was abolished by reorganization in 1977. So Glen truly represents the continuity in Congressional space affairs. Since leaving the Senate, Dr. Wilson has made important contributions to space education and public involvement in space: first, as originator of the NASA Space Shuttle Student Involvement Program, then, as Executive Director of the National Space Society, a position from which he retired several years ago.

Logsdon: Glen, thanks for joining us this afternoon. I think you have a lot to add to the record. Give us, first a sense of the environment surrounding the Preparedness Investigating Subcommittee Hearings. What was the goal of Senator Johnson and of the Hearings? Why were there so many witnesses? There were seventy-three witnesses over the course of the hearings. Was that planned at the start?

Wilson: Well, Sputnik hit Washington quite hard and, as has been brought out already, some people at the White House tended to downplay the achievement. Clarence Randle, who was a special assistant to President Eisenhower called it a silly bauble, and so forth. There are a lot of quotes that I have written in my paper.[2] But they could not keep down the public concern about it. The newspapers, of course, played it up quite vigorously. It was front page stuff practically every day for weeks. You've heard from Gerry Siegel how Senator Johnson first heard about this and really picked up the ball and ran with it. There was no question about who was first in getting on with this job. There have been some people who said Johnson was slow to get started, and the record shows that that is anything but the truth. The truth is that he was the first man to do this. I'm not quite sure that they had decided when they were going to have hearings while they were doing all this conferring during the month of October of 1957, but *Sputnik 2*, which came on November 3, 1957, absolutely made the decision for them, if they had not already. It really reinforced the fact because it weighed so much more than even the first one, which was a shock, because even the first Sputnik weighed almost nine times more than the one that we had planned to put up. So there was a feeling of excitement and of crisis because of the military security angle that we've talked about. I think that when Senator Johnson brought Ed Weisel down, he told him that it is only going to be for a week or ten days. Mr. Weisel duly set up in the Mayflower Hotel and I don't think he thought he was going have to stay there that long. But as they talked to potential wit-

2. Glen P. Wilson. "How the U.S. Space Act Came To Be." April 3. 1992. Appendix B.

Glen P. Wilson was a staff member for the Senate during the Sputnik crisis and participated in the writing of the National Aeronautics and Space Act of 1958 and later served on the Senate Committee on Aeronautical and Space Sciences throughout its entire existence from 1958 until the Senate reorganization in 1977. (NASA photograph)

nesses it sort of grew. They discovered that there were a lot more angles that needed to be looked into. And so they went on with the hearings. Incidentally Mr. Weisel, at first, had said that he wanted to put the hearings off until after the first of the year but I knew when they were going to start—when Lyndon Johnson said they were going to start. They started on the twenty-fifth of November. The timing was just perfect because it grabbed all the attention in the newspapers and television. It hit the public consciousness pre-holiday; it didn't get mixed up in Christmas.

Logsdon: Sputnik, at least in retrospect, was interpreted as a failure of U.S. society, a failure of our education system. It led to the National Defense Education Act. Do you think the Subcommittee's work contributed to the sense that it was not only a Soviet achievement, but a U.S. failure?

Wilson: Well, I think as George Reedy said in his October 17th memo, the idea behind the Hearings was to bring out the facts, not try to look for scapegoats. Let's educate the American people about what's happening here. I don't think that many of us who were there at the time really realized the impact that this was going to have. I mean, the Hearings were held in the famous caucus room in the old Senate Office Building, where a lot of famous hearings were held—the MacArthur Hearings and so forth. Anyway, it was absolutely jam packed in that place. It had lots of attention.

Logsdon: The Committee produced, I think, twenty-three recommendations, three of which had to do with space, and the rest had to with other aspects of preparedness. What would you say were the major impacts of the Committee's work?

Wilson: I believe there were seventeen recommendations. Of the seventeen, three of them related specifically to the space program. The rest of them related to the military or missile program and so forth. But perhaps the one was most closely associated to space called for work to start at once on the development of a rocket motor with a million pounds of thrust. The two other ones involved accelerating and expanding research and development programs and providing funding on a long-term basis and improving control and administration within the Department of Defense, or through the establishment of an independent agency.

Logsdon: So that was considered an option at this point?

Wilson: Yes, absolutely. And then the last one was to put more effort to the development of manned missiles, meaning satellites.

Logsdon: Humans in space?

Wilson: Yes, humans in space.

Logsdon: At that point a separate space agency was considered an option from the Senate's point of view. Was it a preferred option?

Wilson: Well, that wasn't the focus of those hearings.

Logsdon: They weren't concerned with organization?

Wilson: That is correct. It was not a set of hearings designed to ask what kind of Federal organization we needed for all this, although in the hearings the topic came up several times. Nelson Rockefeller was asked directly whether space should be under civilian or military control. He said, "I'll pass on that."

Logsdon: Because it hadn't been decided at that point?

Wilson: That is correct.

Logsdon: Well, you've heard what Gerry Siegel had to say about the Special Committee on Space and Astronautics, of which you were one of the early staff members. What do you have to add to that in terms of getting that Committee organized and up and running?

Wilson: Well, the beginning of January marked a new session of Congress. Everybody who had anything in mind about the space program put a bill into the hopper. Senator Anderson put a bill in to give space to the Atomic Energy Committee. Other Senators put bills in to give it to the Commerce Committee or whatever, and it was reaching a point of near chaos. Lyndon Johnson stepped in on Febrvary 5, 1958, and dropped a resolution in the hopper to create the Special Committee which was a Blue Ribbon Committee. And, again, to emphasize how Mr. Johnson ran things in those days, he introduced it on February 5th; it passed February 6th.

Logsdon: He was, after all, the Majority Leader in addition to everything else.

Wilson: That is right. And Gerald Siegel, of course, was involved. The committee had its first organizational meeting, I believe, February 20th or something like that. There was a period of sort of digesting the bills and so forth.

Logsdon: As far as you know, was there any interaction with the White House? As you probably knew, the Administration was developing a proposal.

Wilson: I can't answer that point directly. Perhaps Lyndon Johnson knew. I did not come on the staff until March the twenty-third, I think it was.

Logsdon: Just a week or two before the Administration bill came up. Describe the dynamics within the Congress and between the Congress and the White House that led, finally, to the July 29th Space Act.

Wilson: The Administration sent the bill down, and it had numerous flaws in it, because it had been done rather hastily. Eilene Galloway, whom you will talk to a little bit later, immediately went to work to analyze the bill. She wrote a very lengthy and perceptive memorandum about the faults in the Administration proposal. Then the House Committee started its hearings, and had a long set of hearings.

Logsdon: Right, because they had not had the investigating background.

Wilson: That is correct. They did not have the background that had come from the Preparedness Subcommittee Hearings. So there was some interaction. But I cannot tell about it, I was mostly a spear-carrier in those days, taking care of the records to see that stuff got to the printers and that sort of business. So I wasn't involved in anything high level.

Logsdon: Let's shift focus a little bit. What about the issues as it became clear that there was going to be a space agency and Congress had to set itself up to deal with this new area of activity and new organization. What were the issues there?

Wilson: Well, this is a very interesting story. As you've heard, the members of the House Committee had in mind something that was more like the Atomic Energy Commission, although that was ultimately dropped from the bill. That carried over then to how they were going to handle it in the Congress, and so they proposed a Joint Committee. It was

19

a very powerful committee, the Joint Atomic Energy Committee, and they wanted to duplicate that. The bill that passed the committee unanimously with a Joint Committee in it, but something happened between there and the time it got to the House floor. That something, I believe, was a phone call from Lyndon Johnson to Sam Rayburn. They talked every day, anyway. Mr. Rayburn was well known for being opposed to Joint Committees. I think Mr. Johnson must have brought it to Mr. Rayburn's attention that there was a Joint Committee in that bill was coming up on the House floor. As a consequence of that, that provision was dropped as a Committee amendment on the House floor. In the meantime, the staff of our Committee had been looking at the work that the House Committee had done and it had a Joint Committee in it. So when we met for our mark-up session, we had in our drafts a provision for a Joint Committee. But the House had taken it out. Lyndon Johnson insisted on keeping it in there. He said, I need something to bargain with.

Logsdon: In the Conference Committee?

Wilson: Yes. Of course, that's exactly the way it worked out. But Johnson didn't want a Joint Committee. He didn't like to share things like that with somebody else. He wanted a Committee of his own. He was like a chess player. He could see several moves ahead, and he knew that he could get what he wanted this way. meaning a regular Committee of his own, and have something for himself as well, which was the National Space Council.

Logsdon: Right after the Space Act was signed July of 1958, almost as a first amendment, there was a requirement for annual authorization of the NASA budget. What was the background of that?

Wilson: Johnson had been on the Appropriations Committee. He knew how the Appropriations Committee could cut an agency up by taking money away; they control the money flow. He also knew that if you could go before the Appropriations Committee and show that you have really looked into these various programs, there was much more reluctance on the part of the Appropriations Committee to cut it back. So he decided to work this out with John W. McCormack, the House Majority Leader and the Chairman of the House Space Committee. They just said we'll make this so that all the money has to be authorized first, thereby giving the agency a much better means of getting their money out of the Appropriations Committee. But Mr. McCormack left town on his August vacation in New England and he failed to tell the members of his Committee of the deal that he had made with Senator Johnson. So, it went sailing through the Senate, of course, and when it got to the House, the people from NACA had spent a lot of time massaging this issue with their friends on the House side; Paul Dembling can tell you about this. They got up and made all sorts of reasons why NASA shouldn't have to come and do this every year. Well, Johnson was furious about this because he'd made a deal with McCormack and McCormack had not passed the information along to his own Committee members. So when McCormack finally got back they settled it. They said we'll make this good for one year only, but then, of course, by the next year it became permanent. NASA profited by that for many years.

Logsdon: I know there is lots more to be added, but we're out of time. We'll get back together in a little while. Thank you very much.

Wilson: Thank you.

Conversation with H. Guyford Stever

Guy Stever *has been a central player in almost every issue of U.S. science and technology policy over the past four decades, so it is no surprise that in 1957 and 1958 he was in the middle of discussions over how best to organize the U.S. space effort. Guy has been President of the Carnegie Institute of Technology, Director of the National Science Foundation, and was Science Advisor to President Gerald Ford. Since leaving government, he has been active in an staggering variety of advisory committees. Back in 1957 and 1958, Dr. Stever, who at the time was an MIT faculty member, was working with both the Air Force and the National Advisory Committee for Aeronautics as those organizations tried to decide how to position themselves in the new space arena. Dr. Stever testified to both the Senate and House Committees set up to consider the Administration's Space Act proposal. It's an honor to have him join us today.*

Logsdon: Guy, you were closely involved at the time of Sputnik with those in the Air Force that thought that defense requirements should receive priority in organizing the U.S. space program. Talk a little bit about the Air Force point of view at that time.

Stever: John, as in every large organization there were many points of view in the Air Force. They were determined, of course, to get the necessary space programs to carry out their important missions in defense. If these missions helped scientific exploration and other science work, they would go along with them. But I think that the priority on the defense parts of the missions was important. You must remember that when Sputnik came along, it was a surprise to most people in the nation, but it wasn't a surprise to many in science and technology, aeronautics and, later, astronautics.

Logsdon: It had been clear that Sputnik was coming to those in the know or paying attention.

Stever: That's right, and, in fact, there were battles, long before Sputnik, within the Department of Defense and the Air Force, as to whether they should get involved in helping the scientists send up instruments into space or to very high altitude in the atmosphere. So there were lots of divisions of opinion on that. I think that at all times the Air Force and other services were going to defend the right to have a high priority, not necessarily the highest, for military space. And, by the way, they have had it ever since.

Logsdon: Of course, there were some in the Air Force that began hatching plans for putting humans in space, space exploration, more or less rationalized under defense requirements even at those early days.

Stever: Absolutely, and the people who were very anxious to stick to the surface warfare—if you include ballistic missiles in surface warfare—they wanted to avoid getting too overwhelmed. But, of course, space did offer some remarkable military capabilities in reconnaissance and communications. Most of space is now used by the military.

Logsdon: I think that's been recognized from the very start. Now, at the same time, you had this National Advisory Committee for Aeronautics, that had been set up during World War I to be the research agency for the nation's aeronautics sector, that was interested in what it should do with respect to space. You were asked by General James A. Doolittle, the Chairman of the Committee, to help think that issue through. Talk a little bit about that.

Stever: Yes, Jimmy Doolittle, who was also Chairman of the Air Force Scientific Advisory Board, (I was Vice-Chairman) had been interested in space for some time and asked me, right after Sputnik, if I would head a group making a study of what NACA had to do to become a space agency. I told Jimmy that he had already assigned me to two major Air Force studies, and, for a month or two, I was going to be quite busy, but then I would be glad to do it. So he said that he would put it off. About the end of 1957 or early 1958, we began this NACA study, which was essentially to figure out what was needed in space in the way of science and technology, and to determine, then, what NACA did not have and needed to become that agency.

Logsdon: By that time had NACA gotten some glimmer that it was going to be the core of the new agency, or was it still one of the contenders?

Stever: Oh, I think it was one of the contenders at that time, but many people pushed for it. It was a civilian government agency. I think that there were some in the university world that would have preferred something quite different than NACA to do the work.

Logsdon: Something like working through the National Academy of Sciences of the National Science Foundation (NSF)?

Stever: Yes. There were lots of proposals. I think it soon began to emerge that it had to be a government agency, and a big government agency. If you wanted a civilian one, NACA did have lots going for it, and a good number of the technologies.

Logsdon: In these deliberations both within the Air Force and NACA, was the Congress at all influential in emerging Congressional views, or was this really Executive branch business?

Stever: I think Congress was very active, viewed from my position at MIT as opposed to my position at the Air Force. In Washington, the statements were flying thick and fast. It was hard to sort it out from a distance. The power structure began to emerge, and it was soon evident that Senator Johnson was going to have a very powerful role, which led to my getting involved in testifying to his Committee and the House Committee.

Logsdon: The Administration put a bill forward and both the Senate and the House held hearings and you testified to both of them. What kind of message were you trying to bring at that point?

Stever: Well, it was the first time I'd testified to any member of the Congress who was as powerful as Senator Johnson. It was quite interesting because Hugh Dryden asked me if I would go to testify.

Logsdon: Hugh Dryden was then the Director of NACA.

Stever: Yes, he was Director of NACA, and testified first, then I did. They ripped him apart. Now, the reason was that the Congress was upset and had been ever since the end of World War II, that NACA had dropped behind, particularly the Germans, in the development of high-speed aircraft, supersonics, jet engines, and so on. There was a running battle going on even before Sputnik about that. So they always liked to take NACA representatives apart based on that. Hugh had a little bit of trouble. I was sitting there wondering, what's going to happen to poor little me, a professor from MIT. Senator Johnson treated me just as well as I could possibly be treated. We had a good show and all the others did not. I spoke to Hugh afterwards. He said that was the difference between somebody who works for the government being asked questions and somebody who does not.

Logsdon: Did you get a sense of the forces that were operating at that point? The Administration had put forward a bill setting up a civilian agency. I don't think there was unanimous support for that approach.

Stever: The difference between something like the Atomic Energy Commission versus a converted NACA versus some other units, people thought that they might take some of the military units and set up a brand new agency. I think there was a great deal of creative, institutional thinking, but I think NACA emerged fairly quickly.

Logsdon: Did you get involved in any of the decisions on which programs to transfer that had been, for example, Air Force programs, to the new agency?

Stever: Well, the first big transfers, of course, were from the Army, and that was the Huntsville Redstone arsenal units with Wernher von Braun.

Logsdon: Well, that took a little fighting. That didn't happen until 1959.

Stever: I know, but that was the big transfer. By the way, von Braun was on the NACA Committee.Both he and Pickering seemed a little bit reluctant in the discussions. But,

Dr. William H. Pickering, director of the Jet Propulsion Laboratory; astrophysicist Dr. James A. Van Allen, University of Iowa; and Dr. Wernher von Braun, director of the Army's Redstone launch vehicle program, announced on February 1, 1958, at the National Academy of Sciences that they had successfully launched the first U.S. satellite, Explorer 1. This was the signature image that appeared in newspapers around the nation the next morning, but this success also served notice that the nation had to codify the authority for space exploration in a single organization. (NASA photograph)

soon they got in the spirit of things. Pickering was then the head of the Jet Propulsion Laboratory (JPL).

Logsdon: JPL was also an Army facility at this point.

Stever: Yes, and so our point was that NACA was good in structures, aerodynamics, and organization, but they weren't good at electronics, and they needed a lot more in rocketry. Those were key transfers. But, there was one other missing link, the need for greater strength in electronics. And, in fact an electronics lab was established by NASA in 1962. By then the electronics industry had begun to fill in.

Logsdon: One Air Force program that was transferred immediately to NASA was manned spaceflight. What ultimately became the Mercury Project had its origins in Air Force planning. Is there any background there that is worth putting on the record?

Stever: Well, I think it was a natural. We couldn't have a civilian space program without manned spaceflight and why not make that transfer. I do not recall any great arguments that centered around that; I'm quite sure there were some, but I didn't get involved with it.

Logsdon: You were an MIT faculty member and presumably were in conversations with Dr. Killian, who was Science Advisor and President of MIT. What was his view? He, later, was rather skeptical of the value of humans in space. Was that a view that Dr. Killian and the scientific community had from the very start?

Stever: Some of them did; some of them didn't. I don't think he was completely against it, but I don't think he was overwhelmed by it either. But, you know, the general populace in the country got very enthusiastic about it. This support was recognized very quickly by anybody who was in politics, but not necessarily in the university world.

Logsdon: Is there anything else you think needs to be added to understand, from your perspective, what went on in those creative twelve months or so?

Stever: No, when I look back on the whole history of my life associated in and out of government, I think it was a remarkable period of taking account of these immense pressures from so many people, positive interests and negative fears from the people.

Logsdon: You mean people not understanding what this all meant?

Stever: Absolutely, to convert that to an agency, I thought, was a great accomplishment. By the way, there were other great accomplishments attendant to Sputnik. People felt that Sputnik proved the need to strengthen our weak education. So, it was, all in all, a source of pride that our battling came out with a positive construction.

Logsdon: Thank you very much for being with us.

Stever: Thank you.

Conversation with Paul G. Dembling

*I'm pleased to note that our next guest, **Paul G. Dembling**, received his law degree at the George Washington University. Paul went to work for NACA in 1946, and by 1958 was the organization's top lawyer, its General Counsel. Once the White House had decided that NACA would serve as the core of a new space agency, Paul played a central role in drafting the legislation that the White House sent to the Congress in April. Then he was one of the links between the Administration and Congress in resolving differences between the Administration's Senate and House Space Bills. Once NASA became operational, Paul joined the staff, eventually becoming NASA General Counsel. And, later, he served as the General Counsel of the General Accounting Office. Since leaving public service, Paul has been one of the founding partners of a major Washington law firm.*

Logsdon: Thanks for joining us today, Paul. Before President Eisenhower settled on NACA as the foundation for a new space agency, there was a lot of competition among various agencies for that role. What were some of the issues and reasons that NACA was chosen?

Dembling: As some of the others have indicated, there was a lot of competition. The Air Force felt that it should be the agency to do all space research and to be the operating space agency. The Atomic Energy Commission felt very strongly that, if we were going to go into space, nuclear power was going to put us there, and therefore it should be the agency to assume the role. NACA had done a considerable amount of space research, as Guy Stever pointed out. He was there to assess what NACA had done, and was doing, and what was needed to continue its role as the space agency. Soon after the Russians had launched Sputnik there was a group of individuals in NACA that felt NACA should be much more aggressive in either assumming the role it should be playing, or at least to try to seek the Administration's blessing in that regard. They pressed Gen. James A. Doolittle, who was Chairman of NACA, and Dr. Hugh L. Dryden, who was its Director, to take a much more aggressive role. As a result of those meetings, some very strong, Doolittle and Dryden referred to them as the young Turks in the organization. As a result of some of those discussions, I suggested that I be given authority to draft a bill that we could send up to the Bureau of the Budget for its consideration.

Logsdon: So, this was NACA trying to take the initiative.

Dembling: Yes, the argument that I made to Dr. Dryden and Dr. Doolittle was to recognize that Washington operates on the first draft that it gets, and maybe we might seize the high ground.

Logsdon: Did that happen?

Dembling: It did happen. I was authorized to go off in a corner and draft as much as I could of the kind of organization that would resemble NACA, and would have the authorities necessary for it to be the space agency.

Logsdon: When was this? December-January?

Dembling: The first meeting with the so-called young Turks occurred in October. There was a later meeting in December, and then I sort of went to work in January or early February. There were two considerations: one was, we felt in NACA, that there was enough authority for us to take over the space program. As Willis Shapley pointed out there was a feeling that

25

Paul G. Dembling was the general counsel of the National Advisory Committee for Aeronautics (NACA) during the critical 1957–1958 period and played a principal role in drafting the bill which ultimately became the National Aeronautics and Space Act of 1958. He later served as the NASA general counsel. (NASA photograph)

there were enough authorities; it was just the blessing of the White House and the Congress that was needed. However, from a political standpoint, we recognized that the populace was demanding real action. And if the real action was to set up and create a new agency, we wanted to be the foundation on which that agency was going to be built.

Logsdon: You started interacting, I would presume, with the Bureau of the Budget, with Willis Shapley, pretty early on in this period?

Dembling: We interacted early on with the people in the Bureau of the Budget and we started to interact with the Congress because we knew that the other agencies were trying to persuade the Congress that they should be the ones.

Logsdon: Who were you talking to in the Congress?

Dembling: Well, we were talking to members of the Committee the Majority Leader, Senator Johnson, had established. To give you a feeling about the political environment as it existed at that time, when we tried to see Senator Styles Bridges, who was the ranking minority member of that Special Committee, he didn't want to see us on the Hill. He said, he did not want to be accused by the Department of Defense of meeting with civilian agency representatives. So we met on neutral grounds, which happened to be a suite in the Hotel Carlton. This was a suite that a president of a company always took when he came to town. We would relay our messages to him to meet with Senator Stiles Bridges and he would relay them to the Senator.

Logsdon: So this was not exactly a low pressure situation?

Dembling: It was not a low pressure situation. We also recognized that others were trying to persuade lots of people on the Hill.

Logsdon: Ultimately, in the Executive Office of the White House, a decision was made, embodied in this March 5 memorandum, to build a new agency around the core of NACA. I guess then you became part of the central team?

Dembling: That's right.

Logsdon: You were part of the team putting together the legislation to put that into practice. Talk about that period.

Dembling: Well, there were five of us that worked on the legislation, using the draft that I had submitted. There were other aspects that had to be included. Bill Finan, who Willis Shapley mentioned, was the coordinator of the group. Alan Dean came from the Bureau of the Budget. Ken McClure, who was Assistant General Counsel of Commerce, was a detailee from that organization, and Paul Johnson, who was a member of Dr. Killian's staff, came over on loan from the Institute of Aeronautics and Astronautics.

Logsdon: What was the balance between, if you wish, the new Science Advisor's operation and the BOB in influencing the outcome?

Dembling: The prime influence, I thought, was that Killian had stated that it ought to be a civilian agency. I understood that Killian convinced President Eisenhower that that was the route to take.

Logsdon: What were the major issues that were embodied in the Administration bill? Were they pretty much the ones that were in your original NACA-generated draft?

Dembling: All of the terms and conditions on the authorities and the functions that were in the original draft pretty much remained the same.

Logsdon: Presumably, several of those were pretty broad authorities for their day?

Dembling: They were the broadest authorities, and the reason they were broad was that, in my draft, I went through all of the decisions that had been rendered by the General Accounting Office and the Attorney General's Office. All of those decisions spoke about the authorities that agencies did have or did not have. If the decision said that, yes, you can go ahead and do this because you have this authority, I put that into the draft. Of course, conversely, if it said, an agency did not have that authority, because it didn't have the words of art, or the jargon that was necessary to give it authority, I put that in the draft. So the draft that was sent over had very broad authority.

Logsdon: Once the bill got to the House and then the Senate began hearings on it, how much lobbying was there on the part of the Administration? Was there an issue of the bill not being supported or was the question maintaining the major provisions of the Administration approach?

Dembling: I think the major point was that the concept had to be agreed upon. I don't think that was very difficult to agree that it should be a civilian agency. Initially, if you recall, NACA operated with the Board of Directors, which was called the Committee. It is a misnomer to say it was advisory.

Logsdon: No, it was kind of a line authority.

Dembling: It had the Board of Directors, with the head of that being Dr. Doolittle. By the way, while known as General Doolittle, the head of the Eighth Air Force during World War II and as leader of the group that bombed Tokyo, he had an eamed doctorate in science from MIT. So we always referred to him as Dr. Doolittle.

Logsdon: Not General Doolittle?

Dembling: No, not General Doolittle. He coordinated the activities of the so-called Board of Directors. Then Dr. Hugh L. Dryden was the operating head of the organization, the day-by-day operations, sort of the Chief Executive Officer or a president of a company.

Logsdon: There was a set of interactions as the House and Senate suggested modifications to the Administration Bill. How much resistance on the part of the Executive Branch was there?

Dembling: Actually, there was little resistance to any of the additions or changes that were made. There was some consideration given to making sure that the authorities to be included were broad enough, primarily to assure that those agencies engaged in space research could be transferred over to NACA.

Logsdon: How about the Administration? I think they had pretty strong resistance to the idea of something like a Space Council or a top-level advisory board, and yet, ultimately, agreed to that. Did you get involved in that set of negotiations?

Dembling: Yes. Senator Johnson felt at the time, as we understood it, that there ought to be a strong voice in the White House similar to the National Security Council. Therefore, he felt that the Council would coordinate the work. The way he sold it to the Administration, finally, was to state that the Chairman of the Space Council would be the President, and, therefore, it was all right. You recognize that, later, when he became Vice-President the legislation was amended to make the Vice President Chairman of the Council.

Logsdon: Finally, let's talk a little bit about the international dimensions of the Space Act that, in Section 205, gave authority to the new agency to carry out international programs, and that, apparently, caused some legal problem on the Administration's end. Can you talk a little bit about that?

Dembling: The original draft that was considered and discussed with the State Department did contain a provision similar to what was finally adopted by the Congress.

Logsdon: But this provision didn't make it in the bill.

Dembling: No, because the State Department objected. They convinced the White House that it should not be included because foreign policy was decided by the President. It was felt that including that provision in the bill would give NASA authority that the State Department should have. And so, if you'll recall, when President Eisenhower signed the bill, that became the NASA Act, he took a reservation on that provision and said that he understood and was intetpreting it as not affecting foreign policy direction of the President and, of course, the State Department.

Logsdon: Paul, over your career, you've seen a lot of legislation. How would you rate the Space Act? It seems to have lasted very well. Why do you think that's the case?

Dembling: It was done in a hurry; a lot of the policy aspects of it were done quickly. But the functions and the authorities that were embodied in that piece of legislation were well thought out and very well considered. Let me just give you one example that typifies the rest of the bill. If you'll notice, all of the functions are carried in the name of the Administration. They are carried in the name of NASA, not in the name of an Administrator or a Secretary, as most pieces of legislation do. Usually, if they are carried in the name of an individual position, it creates delegation problems, problems of whether an Administrator can delegate authorities to people below him. We did not have that problem in NASA. Because all of the functions that the Congress embodied in that Act were given to the Administration. So the Administrator could place those functions anywhere he wanted within the organization. It gave flexibility to the Administrator that was quite rare. Immediately after the NASA Act, the Federal Aviation Act was drafted.

Logsdon: It followed that model?

Dembling: Yes, it was based on that model.

Logsdon: Thirty-four years after the fact, we look back at this period of very creative policymaking, and say, that was the way to do it. Thank you very much for being with us, Paul.

Dembling: Thank you.

Conversation with Eilene Galloway

Eilene Galloway *is a true pioneer in the fields of space law, policy, and organization. She joined the Legislative Reference Service of the Library of Congress in 1941, and worked there tirelessly until she formally retired in 1975. Those of us who know Eilene well recognize that she never has actually stopped working day after day. She has a political science degree from Swathmore, which, incidentally, is presenting her with an honorary doctorate later this spring. The Legislative Reference Service, which is now called the Congressional Research Service, provides essential support for the Members of Congress and for Congressional Committees. The senior staff of that Service are world-recognized experts in their areas. That certainly applies to Mrs. Galloway, whose encyclopedic knowledge of space law and policy is admired by all.*

Dr. Eilene Galloway served as Senior Specialist in International Relations (National Security) for the Congressional Research Service. Following the launching of Sputnik 1, she was Special Consultant to Senator Lyndon B. Johnson and to Representative John W. McCormack during congressional hearings on the "Space Act." (NASA photograph)

Logsdon: Thank you for joining us today, Eilene. What was the background that led to your being so intimately involved as Congress considered space issues in 1957 and 1958?

Galloway: Well, I was the National Defense Analyst. I had assignments from the House Armed Services Committee and the Senate, but, mostly, I had been working for almost a year for the Senate Armed Services Committee, and, in particular, for Senator Russell, who was the Chairman. The primary interest at that time was in missiles whether or not we had enough missiles, how good they were, and what the situation was in the Soviet Union. And, before the Sputnik went up, I had also worked for the Committee on the organization of the Department of Defense for the 1947 Act. I was very familiar with the National Security Council, and with the problem caused by interservice rivalries. This Committee was primarily concerned about the military threat when the Sputnik went up.

Logsdon: This is now the Preparedness Investigating Subcommittee?

Galloway: I had written a report called, "Guided Missiles in Foreign Countries," that was published by both the House and Senate Armed Services Committees in the spring of 1957. Anyone on the Hill who had worked on guided missiles was called upon immediately to work on space.

Logsdon: Well, you've heard Gerry Siegel and Glen Wilson describe the work of the Preparedness Investigating Subcommittee, which you also had direct involvement in. Is there anything you'd like to add to their accounts of those two months of hearings?

Galloway: Yes, it was really a very exciting time. The Sputnik went up on a Friday, and early Monday morning Senator Johnson telephoned me. He said that he had talked to Senator Russell, and Senator Russell had recommended me, because I had helped him with a hearing with the Joint Chiefs of Staff. He said, "Eilene, I want to make me a record in outer space, and I want you to help me." So I said that I would. I think my main qualification was that I was not scared of any assignment. So I began immediately working on the problems of the Congress because there was such turmoil there. The only other time that I remember there being such an impact on the Hill was when the atomic bomb went off.

Logsdon: In 1945?

Galloway: Yes, and I had also worked 1945–6 for Senator Brian McMahon, (Chairman of the Joint Committee on Atomic Energy) and had written a report on "Atomic Power; the Issues before Congress," so I was familiar with that. It was coincidential that a number of these threads of different assignments happened to converge at that time.

Logsdon: So you were the right person for the time. You uniquely worked with both the House Committee and Senate Committee to consider the Congressional reaction to the Administration's space proposals. Give us some of the highlights of your work, particularly, first, with the House Committee and it's Chairman Majority Leader, John McCormack. In particular, I know it was the House that suggested that NASA, which the Administration proposed to be the National Aeronautics and Space Agency, become an Administration. How did that change come about?

Galloway: Well, Mr. McCormack first called me in to ask me whether it was a good idea for him to become Chairman of this Committee that they were thinking of setting up. Originally, it was thought there would be only the Senate Committee because that was the way it had been done with atomic energy. So, I urged him to do it. I said, it was very, very important. Then I said, this was after the bill had come up, I don't like it being called an agency because, it seems to me, that does not have very much status. We have so many agencies of different kinds; we should call it something more important. The whole idea was to get this at the Presidential level and have it sound like a very important organization. So he said, we've already started calling it NASA; and I said, can't we call it an administration and have an administrator? Much to my astonishment, he pressed something on his desk, called somebody in, and said, change the bill: strike out "agency" and "director" and write in "administration" and "administrator."

Logsdon: That's how legislation gets written, I guess.

Galloway: Yes. Then I helped him get Charles Sheldon on the staff, who was an expert in transportation.

Logsdon: Was he with the Library of Congress?

Galloway: Yes. Sheldon was a senior specialist in transportation. McCormack asked me to write a report on the task of the Congress in formulating legislation for space. He opened the hearings with this report. It was at a time when a number of people thought that we could erase "atomic energy," and write in "outer space," and pass an identical bill.

Logsdon: Just use the same approach?

Galloway: This was impossible since atomic energy was a source of energy and space was like a new geographic area that we were going to pioneer. I should add that the Preparedness Subcommittee, on the 21st of November, which was a few days before the hearings started on the 25th, received a report from the Rocket and Satellite Panel, which was chaired by James Van Allen. It had been working on this for about ten years. This report had gone to Eisenhower on October 14th. It was all about setting up a civilian agency protecting the Department of Defense and everything it had to do in a military way, but pointing out how many benefits there were to space, especially communications, meteorology, and navigation. We could not do all those things under the law in the Department of Defense. We had to set up a civilian agency.

Logsdon: So, it had to be a civilian agency.

Galloway: In January, Van Allen got together with George Sutton, who was Chairman of the American Rocket Society, and they produced a report which has so many words in it that are similar to the words that are in the Act, like "leadership," "pre-eminence," and separating from the military.

Logsdon: There are a lot of themes that have been there from the very start.

Galloway: Yes, and they were already there at this time.

Logsdon: What were the highlights of your work, then, with the Senate Committee? What led to the creation of what became the National Aeronautics and Space Council rather than the advisory board the Administration had proposed?

Galloway: Well, the House started its hearings first. I had been going to the hearings in April of 1958 for a number of days. I had the transcript of the hearings, and had prepared questions for McCormack to ask Dryden and General Doolittle. So, I had the bill, analyzing it, and came to the conclusion that a seventeen-man advisory board internal only to

NASA, meeting only four times a year, was paid only for per diem and travel, was not the kind of organization that would have any clout at all over other agencies. They were supposed to cooperate with other agencies. This wasn't just NASA and DOD; this was NASA and other civilian agencies like Commerce, State, and what not. They had not mentioned State Department at all in the hearings. So, they did not have much idea of the role of the State Department, although this was a very international subject. I was familiar with the rivalry between the services and with the fact that we had to have the National Security Council. Now, Dryden had gotten along so well and for so many years with the Department of Defense, that the very idea that they could ever have any kind of dispute, or any trouble of any kind, was just unthinkable to him. He just couldn't imagine it, and was surprised that the question was asked. I had to write this report for Senator Johnson, because Johnson wanted to know how he could improve the bill. Before the Senate hearing started, I had written about the Advisory Board and various other things. I was very concerned over whether the agency was going to be research and development, and also operations, or whether it was not. This was very vague. The wording was quite ambiguous. NASA could have been research and development and operations, but there was a mind-set that came over from the NACA. It was like a shadow in the future, not just because of the words in the law, because we could have amended it if we just thought they were ambiguous. Although, when Cyrus Vance asked the question in the hearing, he was told that NASA was an operating agency. This caused trouble all along the line.

Logsdon: So, you were able to convince Senator Johnson that there needed to be some top-level policy coordinating board that had authority over the total national space program?

Galloway: The whole point was that we needed a total United States space program: military and civilian. This wasn't something that we wanted fragmented. We could see that there were lots of parts, and the whole idea was to identify the problem as one of coordination. This cannot be done with an internal board.

Logsdon: Clearly, Senator Johnson took your advice to heart, and was very serious about the role of the Space Council. He insisted on it in the bill, and I guess, eventually, was able to convince President Eisenhower to accept it. Did you get involved in those discussions? Or was that mainly at Senator Johnson's or the Presidential level?

Galloway: I think that was at the Presidential level. My conferences were with Johnson, personally, in dealing with this. Now, this idea could not have taken root in the House, although I was talking to McCormack, who had changed the name of the agency. I had no clout with McCormack with regard to the Space Council. The reason that there was such fertile soil for it in the Senate was because of their interest in national defense. They all knew about interservice rivalry. You did not have to explain it very much; they knew that right away, especially Senator Symington.

Logsdon: If space was going to be important, it needed this kind of coordination.

Galloway: Now, I must say I called it a Board, because it had been called a Board in the bill that came over; it was changed to Council in the Conference Report.

Logsdon: What were some of the major issues in bringing the House and Senate Committee bills and views together? That was one of them, I suppose. There was also the question of this joint Congressional Committee versus separate Committees.

Galloway: Yes, well I was asked to write a report on how the Congress should be organized. I had four options. They were options that I discussed, according to the Congressional Research Service style, in pro and con fashion. One of them was to turn it all over to the Joint Committee on Atomic Energy. Another was to set up a Joint Committee on Space or distribute bills when they came to the Senate and had to be referred to the Committees that were already in existence. This was a subject of interest to Foreign Affairs, Foreign Relations, Commerce, and Agriculture.

Logsdon: What about Armed Services?

Galloway: All of them. The other option was to set up separate Standing Committees. As Glen Wilson has explained, they finally set up separate Standing Committees.

Logsdon: Well, I know lots can be said on the following question. We may not have time to finish all we have to say on the international events in the Space Act. I think that was an area, clearly, where Congress took the lead, pointing out the need for space to be truly international and that was written into the Space Act in Section 205. Talk about some of the background of getting that included.

Galloway: When the bill came over, the Declaration of Policy and Purpose said that the United States should cooperate with nations and groups of nations. And it was apparent that this was an international subject. Right away we needed international tracking stations; satellites went around the globe in ninety minutes or less and over national boundary lines. We had some kind of a relationship with the Soviet Union and were going to have a relationship with the United Nations. There was the role of the State Department, because space technology was a wonderful tool in many ways to use in the conduct of U.S. foreign relations. So, it was clearly international. However, this point was brought out by a number of people in the House and in the Senate who worried about it. I worked with Senator Symington on this. The people in the Executive Branch did not want to have anything more in the bill. We did not have a Section 205, and the Senate, particularly, wanted to put in Section 205. So, we had a meeting of the Senators, all sitting around a table, and the staff was sitting on the side. It had been written down to a certain point. Well, Senator Green was Chairman of the Senate Foreign Relations Committee, and he was apparently asleep. He looked to me to be sound asleep. All of a sudden, just as we were about to agree on the wording, just before the end, he woke up and said, by and with the advice and consent of the Senate. That would apply to all international cooperation. Well, I was absolutely stunned and very, very upset, because I knew that NASA could not have a program of international cooperation if everything had to come to the Senate. So, I spoke to Senator Johnson about this, and he said it was all right for me to tell Herbert Reis, who was in the Office of Legal Affairs in the State Department, of my concern. I think it must have been Herbert Reis who wrote the statement by President Eisenhower, who said that this section does not preclude less formal arrangements. Just a few years later, Senator Symington and Margaret Chase Smith got very excited because they thought NASA was doing more than it should. So I had to get out a Senate document in which I reviewed all kinds of international agreements NASA had, and wrote an introduction on the differences between memoranda of understanding, agency to agency agreements, Executive agreements, and treaties. When you go through it, you can see that there are a lot of things that you can do internationally that do not require an Executive agreement or a treaty.

Logsdon: Sure. Maybe at the end we will spend a couple of minutes on the speech that Senator Johnson gave before the United Nations in November of 1958, in which he highlighted the U.S. position on the need for international cooperation in space. I know you were involved in that.

Galloway: Oh, that was very exciting. Glen Wilson and I were in San Francisco attending a space medicine conference.

Logsdon: Was it in San Francisco or San Antonio?

Galloway: Oh yes, San Antonio, Texas. President Eisenhower asked Lyndon Johnson to go to the United Nations and make a speech which showed that the Executive and Legislative branches were unified in promoting space for peaceful purposes, for the benefit of mankind. So, Senator Johnson with a bevy of people came to San Antonio and took us out to the ranch. We began working on this speech with some other people: Horace Busby, I think, was involved. The rest of us added things and Eisenhower sent down the plane. We flew to New York, where we were met by Henry Cabot Lodge, who was the U.N. Ambassador at that time. We had nineteen other countries lined up. Johnson made this speech in which he said outer space is unscarred by conflict, it must remain peaceful. It must be an arena for peace. It was really an exciting moment because this led the United Nations to adopt the ad hoc Committee on the Peaceful Uses of Outer Space. Within a year, the Soviet Union, Czechoslovakia and Poland had decided to go in with us. We had decided by that time to make all the decisions by consensus instead of voting. So, the full Committee on Peaceful Uses of Outer Space was established and has two Subcommittees, Scientific and Technical and Legal. (The Legal is meeting right now in Geneva.) It began with twenty-four members and now has fifty-three. So, the House was also interested. I should say that I had discussed with McCormack a resolution on international cooperation in space, especially with the United Nations. This passed both the House and the Senate in a concurrent resolution.

Logsdon: Eilene we've run out of time. There's so much more we could say. You've made remarkable contributions to the world's space activities, and particularly in the period we've discussed today. Thank you very much.

Galloway: Oh, thank you.

Roundtable Discussion

Logsdon: We have brought all seven of today's participants together for this final part of our workshop with the idea of filling in any gaps that haven't come out in the conversation so far, checking one another's points of view, because there have been some discrepancies along the way, and, in general adding to the record that we're trying to create. My job is to steer this conversation but, hopefully, a very minimal amount. One area that nobody has mentioned, just to put it on the table, is the impact that some have claimed of President Eisenhower's concern about the ability of reconnaissance satellites to perform overflight and do it without claims of national sovereignty. Did that get into the deliberations of a civilian space agency at all? Or are the historians like Walter McDougall that have made such a point of that missing the point? Do any of you in remembering those discussions view that as an issue at the time?

Dembling: It was not an issue at the time, only because there had been some reconnaissance flights. I must remind the group that NACA was the front for the U-2 operation that the Central Intelligence Agency ran. Ostensibly it was a project which sought meteorological data, but actually was U-2 flights that went over Russia. You recall, later, Gary Powers was shot down.

Logsdon: Indeed.

Dembling: President Eisenhower had to make the explanation.

Logsdon: That was a couple of years later?

Dembling: That was a couple of years later, but it was on everyone's mind. You recognize that Dr. Dryden, who was the Director of NACA, became Deputy Administrator for NASA and was fully aware of that program. One of the first things he did with the first Administrator was to brief him on that issue.

Logsdon: Did this concern, not about military uses, but national security uses of space, enter into the Congressional debate at all?

Reedy: It entered into many of the conversations. I think that it was fairly well realized that this could be aterrific reconnaissance instrument. I think that it didn't enter into our discussions because what could we do about it? You knew it was up there. Nobody really seriously thought about trying to build some sort of missile to shoot them down. The only way it could have entered into the discussions was whether this possibility might mean it should be under wraps, but even that was silly, really.

Logsdon: Eilene, did this issue of satellite overflight get mentioned anywhere in the discussions of what to bring before the United Nations?

Galloway: I think later on it did. In the early months, I don't recall it coming up in that connection. The reason it came up was because of the issue of sovereignty. Planes were operating in sovereign air space. It was legal for the Soviet Union to shoot down the U-2. That was one of the reasons why they didn't want to have any sovereignty in outer space. They didn't know where air space ended and outer space began. Nevertheless, they knew that anything that was in orbit was in outer space. Since these satellites went around in

With the passage of the National Aeronautics and Space Act of 1958, and NASA's establishment on October 1, 1958, President Eisenhower appointed T. Keith Glennan (right) as administrator and Hugh L. Dryden (left) as deputy administrator. (NASA photograph 58-ADMIN-1)

	ninety minutes or less they just automatically went over national boundary lines. They couldn't do anything about that.
Logsdon:	No, not at this early point.
Galloway:	Later on it came up in the U.N. because of the clarity of the pictures that would be taken.
Logsdon:	Yes, but that was many years later.
Reedy:	There was some discussion by the public that I think should be noted here. I think one of the things that bothered a lot of people was the thought that somebody up there with a pair of field glasses could be looking down at them and reading their mail. At one point there was an extreme right wing conservative push. Somehow they got the idea that we were going to wind up with a great big treaty; like the Antarctic Treaty, and that we would give part of outer space and part of the moon to the Russians. It was nutty sort of stuff, but, nevertheless, it was there.
Wilson:	There was the Eisenhower proposal for Open Skies.
Logsdon:	Which was 1955, I believe.
Wilson:	Right. But there was no feasible way to do that in 1957 or 1958. Even the development of reconnaissance satellites did not really take place until the sixties. By that time, the

problem was about where aerospace ended. There was a lot of air law about whether you could fly and where you couldn't, and where outer space began was fuzzy. That is why every place in the Space Act you'll see the term aeronautical and space.

Logsdon: Right.

Dembling: They're paired together because we didn't know how to define the differences. It was also recognized that there was no consent sought to launch any satellite. And none was given. That was the policy that was followed in the United Nations.

Wilson: This is a beautiful example of how reality determines what the law is going to be. I mean the satellites went up; they circled the Earth; they crossed all of the boundaries of various countries. Just *de facto* overflight in space became okay.

Stever: There are still some problems, for example there are limits to how much nuclear material you can put in space. That's because people don't want a lot of crashes with nuclear material being released.

Shapley: Also, John, on the Administration's side, we did a good deal, purposely, to help fuzz the whole idea of where outer space began. We had a big campaign against the French when they argued for eighty kilometers for the boundary. This was a policy idea that we got all the other countries to gang up against. We and them could not afford to be bound by a definition there, because as Glen said, it would not work. The first weather satellites showed the world for the first time that you could really see things from space. It was a great coup and a great thing for the world because the Russians did not object. This was the crucial time when the Russians first accepted the fact, (and other countries would also know) that the U.S. could look at the Russians and vice versa. This was what really set up the possibility of stabilization of the nuclear arms race in later years.

Wilson: What Eisenhower wanted was Open Skies.

Logsdon: Let me try a very different set of questions. Listening to all of you talk as you have this afternoon, it's clear that you have slightly different perceptions of Senator Johnson's attitudes, beliefs, and ideas at this time. George, you've said that he had to be convinced of the importance of space beyond its direct military significance.

Reedy: Right.

Logsdon: I think that others have suggested that he saw the importance of space almost from the very start. So, maybe we can put in a little more texture on what Senator Johnson's ideas were.

Reedy: Let me make one point about Senator Johnson that I think is important in trying to determine his attitude. And that is you were never quite sure what he was thinking. Gerry and I had this experience a number of times. You give him a memo and he would almost immediately come out against it. Now, I'm not sure, in my own mind, that he was really against it. What he was trying to do was see if he could not get something else out of you. In this particular case, I'm reasonably convinced, that he was just thinking at the time of the military importance of it. You know, we were down on the ranch, pretty well isolated. The Austin *American Statesman* did not carry the same kind of analyses of what had happened that we might get out of the *New York Times* or the *New York Herald Tribune*. I think that he may have started out not so much opposed, but with a feeling that this was nonsense: let's get on down to these rockets.

Wilson: Well, I'll make the comment, however, that during those hearings, both the Preparedness Hearings and then later on the bill, every single thing that we know today about the space program came out as a possibility. I mean, you know, the weather satellites, the earth observing satellites, the missions to the planets, every single thing that we've seen happen in the last thirty-four years in space was talked about, mentioned, and understood at that time. Communications satellites, everybody knew that that was going to be the first real usefulness of these objects.

Stever: These ideas were known by many scientists, engineers, and military officers, for six-eight years before Sputnik. Sputnik just opened the bottle for all of the ideas to fly out.

Galloway: Well, my understanding was that Senator Johnson was driving this effort. He was doing a lot of other things at the same time; he was working with some people on civil rights. So, it depends on who he was contacting at the time.

Logsdon: One thing you said in your remarks, George, and that has been widely written on in various histories of this period is that LBJ saw space as an issue that could make him President. You go on to say, I think, that he did not make it overtly a partisan issue. I have a two-part question. Did the Eisenhower Administration see this as a political bombshell that would threaten Republican hold on the White House, and dealt with the Democratic Congress in a partisan way, or vice versa? I mean, what were the partisan elements at this point?

Reedy: I did not have a feeling, very frankly, that the Administration was being overly partisan about this in a Democratic versus Republican sense. My feeling was that there was partisanship, in a sense, in that the Administration was thinking in terms of weaponry, of the military program, and the various things that might flow. There was partisanship on the other side of outer space exploration. You have to be very careful as to what constitutes partisanship under the American system. Too many people analyze our political parties as though they were European political parties. And they aren't. Our political parties are, basically, coalitions. And their basic function, in our society, is to reduce the number of candidates so we can get it down to two. I know some Republicans that are much more liberal than any Democrat I can name. In fact, I sometimes think the only real difference between the Republican and the Democratic Party is Democrats have trouble with left-wing crackpots and the Republican Patty has trouble with right-wing crackpots.

Logsdon: Well, in addition to being a person of substance and a concern about the well-being of the country, Lyndon Johnson was a politician, an ambitious politician who would like to have been President.

Stever: One of you mentioned the fact that just after Sputnik went up, there were powerful leaders both in the Congress and in the Administration, even in the Department of Defense, who poo-pooed the importance of this. In fact, the Department of Defense had made a conscious decision in 1956 not to support a big satellite program. Instead, they set up a very small one in Vanguard. That was well before Sputnik. There was a brief period after Sputnik when many of the leaders of this country were saying it was not very important.[3] And then the larger one, *Sputnik 2* went up. It was a weapon-sized device. Then, the whole country knew, their leaders, too, that it was something to be dealt with.

---

3. Editorial Note: See the comments in Wilson. "How the U.S. Space Act Came To Be." third paragraph. for more information on this subject.

Logsdon:	Yeah, I think it is often missed that *Sputnik 2* was almost, or perhaps more, traumatic than *Sputnik 1* because of the sheer size of it.
Stever:	I think *Sputnik 1* was a phenomenon: you could go see it in your back yard.
Reedy:	Well, Sherman Adams sure was poo-pooing it. He was the one that made the remark about Lyndon Johnson playing outer space basketball.
Dembling:	It must be also noted that NACA was spending something like twenty-five percent of its budget on space research at the time that Sputnik went up. And yet, it was afraid to come out publicly and say that because of the criticism it might have on the Hill. One of the reasons that Guy Stever was appointed to head the Committee, was because his presence as the Chairman would lend a lot of credibility to that Committee, and, having the background that he had, they said, let Guy Stever take a look at what NASA/NACA was doing, and what should it do in order to carry forward.
Reedy:	Let me add one other thing that I think should be on the record here. I am not at all sure that, at that particular point, Lyndon Johnson was interested in the Presidency. I think that he certainly was at earlier times and he certainly was later. But, for all kinds of personal reasons, he'd reached one of those points where he began to say, is this whole thing worth it? He was actually, at that point, talking to many close friends about retiring, going into private life. I think he meant it. I think he got over it, thank God. But I think he meant it.
Galloway:	I think that one of the main features of this particular time was that there was harmony between the Executive branch and the Congress. The emphasis on national defense was so strong that it was holding everybody together. People say that when you have a Republican President and Democratic Congress the two can't get together; this is a good example of one time in which they did.
Logsdon:	The issue was of such national importance it certainly transcended some elements of politics.
Galloway:	When Johnson got to the United Nations, he gave a speech in which he said the President is a Republican and I'm a member of the Democratic Patty; these are distinctions, but they are not differences; we have unity.
Reedy:	That goes back to the point that I made earlier about the nature of our parties. Some regard our government as being parliamentary, which it is not. In the early part of the Eisenhower Administration, Eisenhower's problems were not with the Democrats. We were constantly upholding him against the Republicans.
Logsdon:	The Taft wing of the Republican Party was a very strong isolationist wing. Willis, you look like you want to say something.
Shapley:	I just endorse what the others are saying from the standpoint of us in the Executive branch and in the Executive Office. I never heard the whole thing referred to one bit as a partisan thing. I was not surprised, because during that whole period after the very first couple of years of the Eisenhower Administration the whole atmosphere was not really one of confrontation. You could work not only with Lyndon Johnson, but with George Mahon. The power structure in the House and in the Senate was such that there was basically an accommodation.

Logsdon: They had a national perspective.

Stever: There was another argument, though, going on about military missiles. You remember in the election in 1960, the Missile Gap was a major issue. It wasn't Space Gap, it was those ballistic missiles.

Logsdon: Because that was more clearly threatening?

Wilson: Let me just point out that when Sputnik went up, the very next day we talked about the fact that Lyndon Johnson made calls that very evening to Russell and others. The very next day, Senator Symington sent a telegram to Russell demanding that they have a full meeting of the Armed Services Committee on this. By Monday morning, which was only three days after the Sputnik launch, they were able to tell Symington that the matter had already been taken care of. Lyndon Johnson and Senator Russell decided that Symington would be too partisan in this.

Logsdon: Too shrill?

Wilson: That is correct. That backs up the point you just made here: that there was this feeling that in the hands of Lyndon Johnson, it would be handled in a less partisan way. It would open up the opportunity to put the facts on the table without a lot of "Who Struck John?" stuff.

Reedy: You know, those decisions were made in full cooperation with Styles Bridges, the Chairman of the Republican Senate Caucus.

Siegel: In the face of this rather untalkative group, I want to say prefatorily, that my friends will never believe this if they happened to see this tape, because I have a reputation for never letting anyone finish a sentence. I sat here, and did not interrupt, once. I just want that noted for the permanent record. Now, I would like to say something general about the question of Johnson's role in the early stages of the space program. I think you cannot understand it if you do not understand his unique system of leadership in the Senate. He never introduced a bill that became a major vehicle for passage in any important issue. He would have somebody else introduce the bill. He would lead the Committee through its processes, to the extent sometimes of having to get the bill reported from Committee because the Chairman couldn't quite negotiate it. But he would do this not out in front; he was interested in results. He knew that if he tried to dominate that Senate, in that fashion, he would never be able to pass civil rights legislation, banking legislation, health legislation, and space legislation. And all of the time that we're looking for these gaps of activity in Johnson's role, they were very deliberate examples of his style of leadership. I've had to say this to so many of my friends who said, how could you work for this man. He never passed anything; he never introduced a bill on any subject.

Dembling: Well, that also speaks to the fact that it was a seniority process at the time, which you really don't have now. And, once you lost that, you didn't know who really spoke for the Senate. Of course, a very strong Majority Leader certainly spoke for the Senate, but you knew there were several key figures in the Senate you could go to talk to and know how the Senate was going to operate.

Reedy: When I was on the Policy Committee, quite often I'd pay a courtesy call on the Chairman of the Committee, and then I'd go down and talk to the fourth or fifth man, who was running it. But there's one other point I want to make here: the nature of American politics and government is that of a constantly shifting series of alliances and partisanships. An alliance is formed on an issue. Then the issue changes and, all of a sudden, the people who were in the first alliance scatter, and new alliances are formed. The Johnson genius consisted in knowing what he could put together on any particular issue which might reach clear across the aisle. He even used Joe McCathy a couple of times when he was opposed to Eisenhower by saying to Joe, would you really like to stick it to Eisenhower? I'll never forget that one.

Stever: When he became Vice-President and was appointed the head of the Space Council, didn't he get into a very unnatural environment?

Siegel: Yes, that amendment was his.

Dembling: Something has to be said about that, and maybe this is the time to say it. When he became Vice President, he insisted that the Space Council be under his Chairmanship. He convinced Kennedy. I remember that President Kennedy then called Jim Webb, who was the Administrator of NASA at the time, and for whom I was working. I got the assignment to get a piece of legislation drafted and carried over to the Hill. However, Jim Webb and President Kennedy were concerned about whether Vice President Johnson was going to run the space program. So, Jim Webb and President Kennedy came up with the idea that, okay, we'll send the piece of legislation over; we'll make the Vice President Chairman of the Space Council; but, the President will control the agenda of the Space Council. In that fashion, you can control whether the Vice President, or the Chairman of the Space Council, becomes the head of the space program. And, of course, you see what happened: after a while, the Space Council really did not function completely and really was repealed. When President Bush named Vice President Quayle to head a Space Council, he had to create an administrative Space Council.

Logsdon: In my own research of this period, I note that Johnson took his approach to that role of Vice President of the Space Council in the very early months of 1961. Kennedy asked him to put together the basis for what became the Apollo decision. What Johnson did was to go to the Hill, consult with Styles Bridges, consult with senior Democrats and Republicans in the House, and Senator Kerr, who had taken over the Chairmanship of the Space Committee, and could go back to the President and say, if you propose this, it will be supported in both houses on a non-partisan basis.

Wilson: You may be certain that President Kennedy would never have made that proposal if he didn't know that the slides were greased. I mean, he knew it was going to go.

Stever: I ask the question again: the slides were greased, but didn't the grease get the Vice President into a lower role than he might have played? Wasn't it a downhill greasing for him?

Reedy: I don't think so. You know, one of the problems was Johnson was not a good administrator. In fact Johnson and administrator is an oxymoron. I think in order to run something like the Space Council, you were not administering anything, but you had to know something about administration.

Logsdon: The Executive branch is not the Congress.

Reedy: Right. I think that he was a superb President despite the fact that he got in all that trouble with Vietnam, which he was against, but that's another story. The thing is that when it came to actual management of something, he would step in and manage something that was out of his personal fortune. Thank God Lady Bird would sit back and when he'd lost interest in it, she would step in and put it back together again.

Logsdon: Let me try a totally counter-factual kind of question for you to think about: what if there had been no Sputnik to energize Lyndon Johnson, down on the ranch, to rapid action. As several of you have said, there was a space program born in the United States before Sputnik, and it clearly would have continued in some form. What difference did the galvanizing effect of Sputnik and the involvement of Lyndon Johnson make, do you think, long-term, in what the country has done in space?

Siegel: Crucial, at that time. We would have had to wait for that launching, I think. How fast do you think the program would have gone?

Stever: Well, you know, I've always felt that, as far as our leadership in space is concerned, hadthe Department of Defense decided that we should put up the first satellite, we could have done that. However, if we had launched a satellite, we would not have as big a space program today, simply because, when Sputnik came along, everybody would have said, why get excited?

Wilson: Well, at the time, from when the IGY began on July 1st, 1957, to its end of 1958, in my opinion we might not have even made our commitment to get a satellite by the end of the IGY. You saw how much trouble they had getting the Vanguard up in the first place.

Siegel: The question we really have to ask you, Guy, is, would we have launched, and when, a large satellite that would have produced this perspective.

Stever: Oh, much, much later. I think that Sputnik galvanized the people in this country in all of the activities and a leader in the Congress had to emerge. And Johnson emerged.

Siegel: He was ready.

Stever: Leaders in science, technology, and industry, all emerged at this time. They were all ready.

Logsdon: The country perceived Sputnik as a crisis, and the best in the country responded to it with a rather creative and lasting approach.

Reedy: I think I should add one thing that's been in the back of my mind: a little uneasiness about maybe we went too fast. I know that is not too popular a view. But, nevertheless, would we really have lost anything if the program had proceeded along the orderly lines of scientific research? Obviously, if the Russians put one up, we had to, too. I'm not arguing that at all. I'm assuming that, if it hadn't been for Sputnik, they would not have been any further ahead than we were. We had a missile program that was proceeding just as well as theirs, really. I looked at some of the statistics and, you know, it is true that figures do not lie. Lies can figure. But, I sometimes have a feeling that it went a little too fast. Within a few years, we were looking for excuses. I'll never forget the fall-out thing where we knew we got Teflon frying pans out of the space program.

Dembling: John made a point earlier in talking with somebody; he said, did this not only galvanize the American thinking, but was it also an indication of failure? I think had the Russians, for example, pushed their program and landed on the Moon before we did, this would have certainly had a tremendous demoralizing effect on the American people.

Reedy: Well, I agree to that because we would have had two failures in a row, but, you see, the question was not the Moon, the question was what would have happened if Sputnik had not gone up.

Logsdon: Eilene has been patient.

Galloway: This was a very dramatic incident, this Sputnik, that was a catalyst for every element that we needed to have a space program. We had the scientists and engineers who knew what to do about it. We had the resources. We had an aviation industry that could expand into making space vehicles. We had leadership in the Congress. We had the President and the Majority Leader of the Senate in harmony on what we wanted. We did not have a lot of partisanship. And we found all the benefits that could come from space that could not be done under the law of the Department of Defense. And I think that we would have gone faster. I think that more than some of the others do, because some of the people who were on Van Allen's panel were interested in communications. You see, by 1962, we had the COMSAT act. We had worldwide communications, and the space communications itself was the best benefit that we could have had.

Logsdon: Willis?

Shapley: John, I would like to roll the tape back a little bit to the conditions in which Sputnik galvanized everything else. There had been one step somewhat similar before that. In the mid-fifties, there were various reports that warned how we were falling behind the Russians in missiles. We were scared first about missiles. The conservative Administration was not about to be stampeded by some big military threat; but, the pressure of the Rockefeller and Gaither reports was there. In late 1956, I believe, Eisenhower made the decision to go all out in the ballistic missile area. This had gone from being a dream to a feasible thing because the nuclear scientists had gotten the size of the warheads down so that a reasonable size missile could be an intercontinental missile. So we had already gone through one period of reaction to a Soviet threat, and, while this did not catch the whole of public attention the way Sputnik did, it had been recognized by the attentive public, the people that were concerned knew about it. The country had then seen the large, by those days' standards, amounts of money that were pumped rapidly into all the ballistic missile projects: Atlas, Titan, Thor, and Jupiter. (They were even going to launch a liquid fueled Jupiter from submarines, which would have been one of the hairiest operations ever. Fortunately, that one was changed to the safer solid fueled Polaris program.) So there was, especially within the Defense bureaucracy and the Eisenhower Administration, a precedent when Sputnik came along. They did have a template to follow.

Logsdon: Except the congressional reaction to Sputnik, because it was a public event and, I think, the public reaction was perhaps stronger than it had been to other problems.

Shapley: Absolutely.

Logsdon: The dynamics were very different, I think.

Shapley: The congressional and public reaction was much greater. If you're trying to assay what might have been, it would be interesting to speculate what would have happened if the Eisenhower Administration had gone ahead and pushed more than it did.

Reedy:	Some awful needles were stuck into this thing, though. I can still remember the hearing, where we left with a distinct impression that the Soviets outnumbered us in terms of missiles by an average of about, I think, twelve or fifteen to one. I have forgotten the exact figures. We were giving them credit for having, maybe, fifteen hundred missiles and we were only supposed to have about thirty. It turned out later, after Kennedy took over the Presidency, that we got another look at those figures. The figures had been based on the assumption that the Soviets were manufacturing every missile they possibly could, which they were not.
Siegel:	You know what we need? We need an economic Sputnik to be launched by China to sort of jolt us into getting rid of our present problems.
Stever:	I think it has already been launched by Japan.
Logsdon:	Well, we are getting near the end of our time. Let me turn to each of you and say, if you have another minute or so, is there any one thing you want to make sure that gets on the record that we have not covered today? It's been remarkably interesting and productive. What have we missed?
Logsdon:	Gerry?
Siegel:	I make this flat statement: that, if it were not for Lyndon Johnson, there would not have been a Space Act in 1958. Now, that's not to say it would not have come out in 1959 or 1960. But, with all of the impetus, with all of the fear and concern and with the drives that Sputnik created, it took this man's parliamentary genius to move it so rapidly. He really did move it, not just in the Senate, but in the House.
Wilson:	I would like to add to what Gerry said. It was important that not only was Lyndon Johnson the leader in the Preparedness Subcommittee hearings, and then the Space Committee hearings, but the fact that he was the Majority Leader of the Senate gave him a lot more leverage to get that stuff through and more capability when he was dealing with the House.
Siegel:	But, Glen I want to say this to my Democratic friends today: he was never the Majority Leader. Was he, George? He was the Democratic leader.[4]
Reedy:	There is one point I want to make, and it's on top of what Gerry had to say. I agree with him. I just want to take it one step further. I think that, without Johnson, the launching of Sputnik could very well have led to an increased missile program. I think what really happened here is that Johnson pushed it into the area of outer space exploration. And thank God.
Siegel:	That may not be fair to the Administration. I have discovered just in preparing for these sessions today, that there was, as Guy Stever has pointed out, a great deal of readiness in the Executive Branch to develop some kind of space program.

---

4. Editor's Note: Technically, this was true. LBJ had used as his official title when the Democrats were in the minority in the Senate, "Democratic Leader," rather than "Minority Leader." When the Democrats retook the majority, Johnson continued to be referred to as the "Democratic Leader" rather than "Majority Leader."

Stever: It is a little dangerous for people in a very important segment of our society, like the Legislative branch of our government to underestimate the inevitability of advances in science and technology. When you had ballistic missiles, a satellite was inevitable. Someone was going to do it. I was on a Committee set up by Vannevar Bush in 1948, and we were looking at the time when intercontinental ballistic missiles would be operable. We said 1960. We hit it pretty close as far as operations were concerned. But, at that meeting in 1948, two of our members were already very anxious for us to include the possibility of satellites. The rest of the members were too. But there is an inevitability about it. I agree with you when you said that we would not have had a Space Act as fast without Johnson. He really did coalesce everything. On the other hand, the inevitability of that pressure was there.

Logsdon: Maybe the thing to say in closing, though, is that leadership is taking inevitability and making something creative out of it.

Reedy: Absolutely.

Logsdon: Certainly the Congress and Lyndon Johnson in 1958 did that.

Stever: Yes, I agree with that.[5]

Logsdon: The people that will see this tape or read our proceedings in the future, I think, really have a rare privilege. We have heard from the people that were there in 1957 and 1958 as this very creative period in American policy unfolded. It has really been a privilege for me to sit with you all today. Thank you very much.

---

5. Dr. Stever subsequently added: "In retrospect, many communities have made great advances in space: the research scientists; the military; the industrialists; the explorers; the media; the educators; the students; the public. As we said, it was inevitable."

Appendix A

HOW THE U.S. SPACE ACT CAME TO BE[6]

by Glen P. Wilson

The launching of *Sputnik 1* by the Soviets on October 4, 1957, created a near panic in Washington. After all, the U.S. had announced on July 29, 1955, that we would launch a scientific satellite during the International Geophysical Year, which began in July, 1957.1 Apparently, no one paid any attention to the Soviets when they announced a few days later that they also were going to launch a satellite in conjunction with the IGY.[2] Everyone assumed that the U.S. with its vastly superior technological and industrial capabilities would be first. It came as quite a shock when they weren't.

Lyndon Johnson was on his ranch in Texas (the congress was in adjournment). Gerry Siegel of his Washington staff was there and they immediately discussed the possible impact of this new development. That very night, Johnson was in communication with Solis Horwitz of his staff in Washington and with Senator Richard B. Russell who was at his home In Winder, Georgia. (Senator Johnson, in addition to being the Senate Majority Leader was Chairman of the Preparedness investigating Subcommittee of the Senate Armed Services Committee chaired by Senator Russell). Although Senator Stuart Symington had demanded an immediate full committee investigation, Senators Russell and Johnson had already decided to handle the matter through the subcommittee. By Monday, October 7, 1957, Solis Horwitz had already communicated with Defense Department officials[3] and on Oct. 8 had requested a complete report and arranged for staff briefings which began on Oct. 9.[4] So it is clear that, despite some accounts that "Johnson was slow to respond"[5] the exact opposite was true.

In the meantime, Sputnik was on the front pages in large type almost daily. People were confused and afraid. The announced throw-weight and pinpoint accuracy at putting the satellite in a precise orbit, had profound security implications (because these were also the requirements for long range ballistic missiles). At 184 pounds it was almost nine times heavier than our announced Vanguard. In fact, one British source suggested that in the translation a decimal point had been misplaced and the weight was only 18.4 pounds.[6] There were comments from everywhere and from everybody but some of the most interesting ones were coming from officials of the Eisenhower administration. In an effort to calm things down, there was a clear attempt do downplay the Soviet accomplishment. James C. Hagerty, White House Press Secretary said "We never thought of our program as one which was a race with the Soviets... the satellite launching did not come as any surprise to the U.S."[7]; Sherman Adams, Assistant to the President (today we would call him White House Chief of Staff), said we didn't intend to get into a "game of outer space basketball..."[8] with the Russians, outgoing Defense Secretary Charles E. Wilson called the Sputnik " neat scientific trick"[9]; and Clarence B. Randall, Presidential Advisor on Foreign Economic Policy called Sputnik "...a silly bauble"and that he was "personally very gratified that our nation was not first..." in getting one up.[10]

---

6.   This paper was prepared for the symposium "The Legislative Origins of the U. S. Space Program" jointly sponsored by the Space Policy Institute of the George Washington University and the Lyndon Baines Johnson Library in Austin, Texas. The symposium was held on the George Washington University campus in Washington. D.C.. on April 3. 1992. The paper was subsequently published as "Lyndon Johnson and the Legislative Origins of NASA." *Prologue: Quarterly of the National Archives* 25 (Winter 1993): 362–72.

Even President Eisenhower himself said that the Sputnik didn't bother him "one iota."[11] But some of the members of the President's own party were more than just passingly concerned and Senators Styles Bridges and Leverett Saltonstall, both also on the Preparedness Subcommittee, had joined in with Johnson and Russell to press the Pentagon for explanations on what was really going on with Sputnik and where the U.S. really stood. There was a feeling that it might be necessary to hold hearings in spite of the fact that congress was not in session.

George Reedy [Assistant, Press Secretary (and general factotum as most of us were) to Lyndon Johnson] wrote an extremely perspicacious memo to the Senator on Oct. 17, in which he pointed out the potential political payoff to Johnson, but most importantly, strongly recommended that the "...immediate need is for gathering the facts and presenting them to the public—without hysteria, without elaboration and definitely without partisanship" and, as it developed, looking for solutions for what needed to be done to help solve the problem, rather than looking for scapegoats.[12] Gerry Siegel also notified Johnson that the Pentagon was ready to brief him, Senators Russell and Bridges, which happened the following week.[13]

After the briefing, another bombshell hit on November 3rd. The Soviets launched *Sputnik 2*. Not only did it contain a living creature, a dog named Liaka, but it weighed 1,120 pounds! That buried the skepticism about the 18 pound weight of *Sputnik 1*. Concerns about throw-weight and guidance were intensified. And that settled the matter about when to hold hearings. After another briefing at the Pentagon on November 4th, Johnson announced, with the concurrence of Senators Russell and Bridges, that the Preparedness Subcommittee would begin hearings later that month.[14] He also selected Edwin L. Weisl, a prominent New York attorney and long time friend, to be the Chief Special Counsel. Mr. Weisl brought with him a rising young star from his law firm, Cyrus Vance, and his son, Ed Weisl Jr.

On November 7th, I was transferred to the Preparedness Subcommittee to help in the upcoming inquiry. In addition to regular Preparedness staffers Dan McGillicuddy, Stuart French, and Ben Gilleas, others were brought in from other Johnson staffs as I had been: Solis Horwitz, Gerry Siegel, and Harry McPherson, and Dr. Edward C. Welsh assistant to Senator Symington. Also brought on from the outside as consultants were Dr. William Houston, President of Rice Institute (now University), Dr. Homer Joe Stuart from Cal. Tech., Washington attorney George Bunn, and, most importantly, Eilene Galloway from the Legislative Reference Service of the Library of Congress.

In spite of the efforts of many administration officials to downgrade the Sputnik problem, the Eisenhower administration was seriously concerned and was working behind the scenes to come up with some solutions. In a nationwide television speech on Nov. 7th, President Eisenhower tried to calm the American people, showing them the nose cone that had been shot back from outer space by the Army booster (thus proving the advancement of American technology), stressed the need to give high priority to scientific education, and announced the creation of the office in the White House of Special Assistant for Science and Technology and his intention to appoint Dr. James Killian to this position.[15] This was widely interpreted as an intent by Eisenhower to put a decidedly scientific or "civilian" cast to the upcoming debate over control of outer space exploration. On November 8, the Pentagon announced that, as a back up plan to Vanguard, Wernher von Braun and his team at Huntsville, Alabama, would be allowed to go forward with their plan to launch a satellite using their Jupiter-C booster.[16]

There was a serious concern about the American education system. Was the Soviet system superior? They were turning out more scientists and engineers that we were. Was there something we could do with our educational system that could help us to recover from this setback? I was assigned to look into this problem and wrote several memorandums and letters to leading educators on this subject. The status of our educational system became a major sub-issue in the ensuing hearings and consideration of what we had to do to overcome the Soviet advantage.[17]

On Monday, November 25, 1957, the Hearings of the Preparedness Subcommittee began. Public interest was intense. Johnson grabbed the headlines and TV coverage, as he had planned. But it also put him up-front in the public eye as being "Mr. Space," an Image he held for many years as the one politician who was truly interested in the space program and its implications for the future of the United States and its place in the future development of mankind. His low key "let's not look for scapegoats but let's find out what's wrong and let's do what's necessary to fix it" approach worked very much as George Reedy had recommended. These comprehensive hearings heard 73 witnesses and were printed in three volumes totaling 2,376 pages. There was general agreement: that we could have done better if we had given the satellite project a higher priority; that satellites have military as well as scientific and other beneficial uses; that better organization was necessary; and that we needed to pay greater attention to our technological and scientific education.[18]

There was no consensus (because it was not the primary focus of the hearings) on how the United States should be organized for space activities, although many scientists were strongly urging that a civilian controlled "Space Establishment" be established. Witnesses such as Nelson Rockefeller, for example, while testifying that the Secretary of Defense should decide where space research should be done, opted to "pass," on the question of whether or not there should be an independent civilian agency.[19] The televised failure of the first Vanguard launch attempt on December 6 only reinforced the fact that the United States had a lot of catching up to do. At the end of 1957 it remained an open question of where, in the Federal Government, the responsibility for space development was going to be placed.

During his testimony before the Preparedness Subcommittee on November 27, 1957, Secretary of Defense Neil H. McElroy was questioned about a statement he had made on November 15 announcing his intention to create a position for a manager of antimissile and military space-project developments.[20] This quickly evolved into an addition to the Supplemental Military Construction Authorization Act (HR 9739), creating, within the Department of Defense, the Advanced Research Projects Agency (this was to become PL-325). ARPA was designed to direct long-range antimissile missile and military satellite programs in such a manner as to not detract from other high priority missile programs. After some confusion in both the Senate and the House as to the best way to do this legally, it was finally agreed not to create ARPA by law but to authorize the Secretary of Defense to engage in such "advanced projects" after consultation with the Joint Chiefs of Staff. In conference on the Supplemental Military Construction Authorization Act the following language was adopted: "...and for a period of one year from the effective date of this Act, the Secretary or Defense or his designee is further authorized to engage in such advanced space projects as may be designated by the President". The conference report explained..."This added temporary authorization is included in order to insure that such projects as the Vanguard may continue uninterrupted for the time being."[21]

On January 7, 1958, the second session of the Eighty-Fifth Congress convened. Space was on everybody's mind. There were several bills introduced in the Senate that would have given jurisdiction over space to various committees. On January 23, Senator Johnson presented, on the Senate floor, the points that had been agreed to by the Subcommittee which included "Start work at once on the development of a rocket motor with a million pound thrust," "Accelerate and expand research and development programs, provide funding on a long-term basis, and improve control and administration within the Department of Defense or through the establishment of an Independent agency," and "Put more effort in the development of manned missiles [satellites]."[22] This report, as were all or Johnson's committee's reports was unanimous. This was a steadfast Johnson belief that in matters of national security, and he considered space to be a matter of national security, there were no Democrats or Republicans, only patriots. Not one single Johnson committee report ever contained a "minority view."

At the end of January, just before midnight on the 31st, the country heaved a collective sigh of relief when the Army team, headed by Wernher von Braun, launched the first successful American satellite, Explorer 1. However, at only 31 pounds, it was obvious that we still had a lot of catching up to do.

But the situation in the Senate seemed to be bordering on chaos, and on February 5, Senator Johnson introduced Senate Resolution 256 to establish a Special Committee on Space and Astronautics to frame legislation for a national program of space exploration and development, and to re-refer all bills regarding space to the special committee. It passed without dissent the next day, showing, once again, the mastery that Lyndon Johnson had over the situation.[23] On February 20, to no one's surprise, LBJ was elected Chairman of this new special committee.

On the House floor, in passing the Supplemental Defense Appropriation Act for 1958 (which contained money for ARPA), Congressman George Mahon, on February 6 made the following remarks:

> Mr. Speaker, to go further with reference to this problem of the conquest of space I should say it appears that there is considerable confusion in the Government as to just who is going to handle our growing and urgent programs for the conquest of space. The supplemental budget estimate submitted by the President on January 7, 1958, was based on the Department of Defense being responsible for these programs, specifically those programs having to do with defense. Now we find the President is having a special study made to determine "the type of structure we may need to set up in the field of outer space—as to where it will be in the overall structure of the Government."[24]

On Friday, February 7, 1958, Secretary McElroy announced the establishment of ARPA,[25] although the signing of the Act which gave him this authority did not actually take place until February 12 (PL-325).

In the House of Representatives there was equal concern about how to handle this new element of space, but they felt that they had been put somewhat on the spot by the Senate with the decision to put Lyndon Johnson himself in charge of the Senate Committee. Feeling that it was necessary to have an equally prestigious member to chair its operations, there was great pressure put on House Majority Leader John W. McCormack to take the position. While at first reluctant to take on this additional responsibility, he finally relented and the Select Committee on Astronautics and Space Exploration was created by the House, with Mr. McCormack as chairman, on March 5, 1950.[26] Mr. McCormack selected another prominent New York attorney and long time friend George J. Feldman to be staff director of the new committee. Later, other staff selected were Spencer Beresford, Richard P. Hines, Raymond Wilcove, Harney S. Bogan, Jr., Philip B. Yeager, Dr. Charles S. Sheldon, II from the Legislative Reference Service of the Library of Congress, and Dr. S. Fred Singer, scientific consultant.

Also on March 5, after two failures, *Vanguard 1* was successfully placed into orbit but, with a diameter of 6.4 inches and weighing only 3.25 pounds, it was clearly no match for the Russian accomplishments. This was the satellite that Khrushchev derisively referred to as the "grapefruit."

On March 24, I was transferred to the new staff as was Eilene Galloway, although we had both been working on the "space" problem since November. As before, other people were borrowed from other of Senator Johnson's offices and from other Senators' staffs. Gerry Siegel was the *de facto* staff director, and Ed Weisl and Cy Vance came down to help at the time of the hearings.

Meanwhile, discussions continued within the White House with President Eisenhower, Vice President Nixon, Dr. Killian, and Republican congressional leaders all being involved.[27] Again no consensus emerged in February and, in spite of the passage of PL 325, and the continuing agreement for the high priority of military needs, there still seemed indecision as to the best way to handle non-military projects.

By Wednesday, March 5, the House had created its Select Committee, the situation in the White House had begun to crystallize. In a memorandum to the President on that date, the President's Advisory Committee on Government Organization chaired by Nelson Rockefeller and also signed by Dr. Killian and Budget Bureau Director, Percival Brundage, recommended that long term organization for space exploration be under civilian control and that "...leadership of the civil space effort be lodged in a strengthened and redesignated National Advisory committee for Aeronautics (NACA)."[28]

The President accepted this recommendation, and directed the Budget Bureau to proceed immediately with the preparation of specific proposals for legislative and executive action. This was done and the President sent a message to the Congress on April 2 proposing the establishment of a National Aeronautics and Space Agency into which the National Advisory Committee for Aeronautics would be absorbed.

The new agency was to have responsibility for civilian space science and aeronautical research. It would conduct research in these fields In its own facilities or by contract and would also perform military research required by the military departments. Interim projects pertaining to the civilian program which were under the direction of ARPA would be transferred to the civilian space agency.[29] A 17 member National Aeronautics and Space Board would be appointed by the President to assist him and the director of the new agency. On April 14, the bill was introduced by Senators Johnson and Bridges in the Senate (S.3609) and by Congressman McCormack (HR 11881) and others in the House.

The House committee sprang into action on April 15 hearing 48 witnesses over 17 days ending on May 12, producing a volume of 1,542 pages, and, of necessity, re-covering much of the ground previously covered by the Preparedness subcommittee in November through January.[30]

The Senate committee, sticking mainly to consideration of the language in the proposed bill Itself, conducted 6 days of hearings, May 6–8 and 13–15, hearing 20 witnesses, and producing two volumes totaling 413 pages.[31] Additional urgency wash added to the proceedings when it was announced, on Thursday May 15, the last day of the-hearings, that the Soviets had successfully launched *Sputnik 3* with an estimated 7,000 pounds in orbit.

The House committee, working feverishly, introduced a clean bill on May 20 which was reported out on May 24. Numerous modifications were made from the original proposal, including broadening and clarifying the scope of the space agency, changing its name to Administration instead of Agency, and giving greater authority to the Administrator (instead of Director). It also established statutory liaison committees with the Defense Department and the Atomic Energy Commission and provided for greater dissemination of information and greater international cooperation. It also had a section on patents and created a new Joint Committee on Aeronautics and Space. The bill passed the House on June 2, however, on the House floor, the joint committee was deleted from the bill.[32]

The Senate committee in its deliberations, of course, had the House committee's report before them. The staff had prepared a draft of the bill, with some modifications, for the committee to consider based on the bill reported out by the House committee. Much of the House language was in this Senate draft including the sections on patents and the joint committee. At the mark-up some Senators raised the question of why the joint committee was still in the bill when the House had already deleted this provision. Senator Johnson said he wanted to leave it in so that he would have something to bargain with when it came time for the conference committee.

On June 11 the Senate committee reported the bill out and on June 16 the bill was passed. The Senate version broadened and clarified the scope of the agency, established a powerful Space Policy Board with a staff, authorized a program of international cooperation, and retained the Joint Committee on Aeronautics and Space. Only the patent section was dropped from the bill on the Senate floor.[33]

The White House was opposed to the strong Space Policy Board on the grounds that it would usurp the authority of the President and the House agreed with the Administration. The impasse was broken, however, on July 7 when Senator Johnson and President Eisenhower met at the White House. Johnson proposed that the President himself should be the chairman of the policy board and this was agreed to by Eisenhower.[34]

The House and Senate conferees met on July 15, agreed to the policy board but changed its name to the National Aeronautics and Space Council, rewrote the section on patents, and, of course, dropped the provision for a joint committee. On the same day, Senators Johnson and Bridges introduced a resolution to create a standing committee, the Committee on Aeronautical and Space Sciences, to have jurisdiction over the new agency.

The conference report was passed by both houses on July 16 and, although there was some concern about the international cooperation provision, was signed into law as Public Law 85-568 by the President on July 29, 1958.

The act contained a declaration of policy and purpose; definitions; established the National Aeronautics and Space Council with staff as an advisory group to the President on matters of overall space policy, development of a comprehensive program, allocation of responsibility, and settling of differences; provided for an Administrator and Deputy Administrator; defined the functions of the new agency; established a military-civilian liaison committee; authorized international cooperation; and required reports to the Congress. It also provided for the transfer of NACA and related functions; public access to information; security; patent and property rights and contributions awards; and an authorization for appropriations. To resolve the concern over the international cooperation section, upon signing the act, the President stated, in part:

> The new act contains one provision that requires comment. Section 205 authorizes cooperation with other nations and groups of nations in work done pursuant to the act and in the peaceful application of the results of such work, pursuant to international agreements entered into by the President with the advice and consent of the Senate. I regard this section merely as recognizing that international treaties may be made in this field, and as not precluding, in appropriate cases, less formal arrangements for cooperation. To construe the section otherwise would raise substantial constitutional questions.[36]

On July 21 the House had passed the resolution to create a 25-member standing Committee on Science and Astronautics, and on July 23 the Senate had passed the resolution to create a 15-member standing Committee on Aeronautical and Space Sciences.

In consideration of a supplemental appropriations bill in August, Senator Johnson inserted a provision to require prior authorization for all of NASA's appropriations which was, actually, the first major amendment to the NASA act. This was at first bitterly opposed by officials at the NACA (NASA didn't officially come into existence until October 1) who failed to see how important this would be to them in obtaining appropriations in the future. Through a misunderstanding, it was also opposed in the House. However, a compromise was reached,[37] and the provision made permanent the following year. Because of this provision, NASA received much more money in the ensuing years than they probably would have otherwise.

And in November, in a spirit of rapprochement, The White House asked Lyndon Johnson to make a major speech on space before the United Nations. In his address to the United Nations, given on November 17, 1958, Senator Johnson stressed the importance of conducting space activities for peaceful purposes, emphasized the need for international cooperation, and urged the support of the pending resolution to create an "Ad Hoc Committee on the Peaceful Uses of Outer Space."[38] This resolution was adopted on December 13, 1958.

The entire legislative process, from Sputnik to the end of 1958, was almost a textbook case of how law, spurred by technological advancement, should be made. There is a statement (on p. 141) in Dr. James R. Killian's book *Sputnik, Scientists, and Eisenhower* which sums it up well, except that I have added in italics the words *"the Congress,"* to make it more accurate.[39]

Many influences were brought to bear on the formulation of the [space] legislation, as they should have been, and the final act represented a remarkable blending of the Interests, needs, and objectives of the administration, the Department of Defense, the Congress, and the scientific community. While the President's science advisers had played a key role in opting for a civilian agency and in the shaping of the administration's original legislative proposal, I think they would have readily agreed that their proposals were but the start of a process of developing ultimate legislation that would fairly represent the needs and views of all Interested parties.

Now, in 1992, we are still wrestling with some of the problems of space exploration and development and space organization that were identified during the birth of what is perhaps mankind's noblest adventure. Lyndon Johnson said it best in his opening statement at the hearings before the Special Committee on Space and Astronautics to consider the space bill (May 6, 1958). "Space affects all of us and all that we do, in our private lives, in our business, in our education, and in our Government. We shall succeed or fail in relation to our national success at incorporating the exploration and utilization of space into all aspects of our society and the enrichment of all phases of our life on this earth."[40]

APPENDICES

Notes

1. *New York Times*. July 30. 1955. pp. 8. 9.
2. Statement made by L.I. Sedov. Chairman of the U.S.S.R. Academy of Sciences Interdepartmental Commission on Interplanetary Communications. on August 2. 1955 at a press conference during the International Congress of Astronauts. Reported in Krieger. F. J.A. casebook on Soviet astronautics. RM-1 760. ASTIA Document Number AD 108750. June 21. 1956. (U.S. Air Force Project Rand. Research Memorandum. p. 2).
3. Letter. Solis Horwitz to Senator Richard Russell. October 7. 1957. LBJ Library. Senate Papers. box 355.
4. Letter. Horwitz to Secretary of Defense Neil McElroy. October 11. 1957. LBJ Library. box 355; *Washington Post*. October 9. 1957. p. A3.
5. Robert A. Divine. "Lyndon B. Johnson and the Politics of Space." *The Johnson Years Vol. II* (Lawrence: University Press of Kansas. 1987). p. 217.
6. *Washington Post*. October 7. 1957. p. 1.
7. *New York Times*. October 6. 1957. p. 1.
8. Lyndon Baines Johnson. *The Vantage Point, Perspectives of the Presidency, 1963-69* (New York: Holt. Rinehart. and Winston. 1971). p. 273.
9. *New York Times*. October 9. 1957. p. 1.
10. *Washington Post*. October 22 . 1957. p. A2.
11. *New York Times*, October 10. 1957. p. 1. 14.
12. Memorandum. George Reedy to Lyndon Johnson. October 17. 1957. LBJ Library. Senate Papers. box 420.
13. Memorandum. George Reedy to Lyndon reporting on a phone conversation with Gerald Siegel. undated (but the context of memorandum places it early in the week of October 28. 1957). LBJ Library. Senate Papers. box 420.
14. Lyndon Johnson press release. November 4. 1957. LBJ Library. Statements file. box 3.
15. *New York Times*. November 8. 1957. p. 10.
16. *New York Times*. November 9. 1957. p. 2.
17. "Inquiry Into Satellite and Missile Programs." *Hearings before the Preparedness Investigating Subcommittee of the Committee on Armed Services, U.S. Senate, 85th Congress, 1st and 2nd sessions* (Washington. DC: Government Printing Office. 1958). Part II. pp. 2149–2216.
18. Ibid.. 3 Parts.
19. Ibid.. Part l, pp. 1055–1056.
20. Ibid.. Part l, pp. 217–218.
21. Conference report on H.R. 9739. Supplemental Military Construction Authorization Act. House of Representatives. 85th Congress. 2nd session. February 6. 1958. Report No. 1329. pp. 7-9.
22. *Congressional Record*. January 23. 1958. pp. 805-807.
23. S. Res. 256. creating a Special Committee on Space and Astronautics to frame legislation for a national program of space exploration and development. *Congressional Record*. February 6. 1958. pp. 1551–1553.
24. *Congressional Record*. February 6. 1958. p. 1604.
25. Department of Defense. Office of Public information. News release No. 109–58. February 7. 1958.
26. H. Res. 496. to establish a Select Committee on Astronautics and Space Exploration to investigate the problems of outer space and to submit recommendations for the control and development of astronautical resources. *Congressional Record*. March 5. 1958. pp. 3019–3020.
27. Legislative Leadership Meeting. the White House. Supplementary Notes. February 4. 1958. Eisenhower Library.
28. Memorandum for the President. March 5. 1958. Subject: Organization for Civil Space Programs. Executive Office of the President. President's Advisory Committee on Government Organization. Eisenhower Library.
29. *Congressional Record*. April 2. 1958. pp. 5489-5490.
30. "Astronautics and Space Exploration." *Hearings before the Select Committee on Astronautics and Space Exploration, U.S. House of Representatives*. 85th Congress. 2nd session. on H.R. 11881.
31. "National Aeronautics and Space Act." Hearings before the Special Committee on Space and Astronautics. United States Senate. 85th Congress. 2nd session. on S. 3609.
32. *Congressional Record*. pp. 8892–8918.
33. Ibid.. p. 9829.
34. Johnson. *Vantage Point*. p. 277.
35. Conference report. H. Rept. 2166. agreed to in the House and the Senate (Congressional Record. p. 12737).
36. Dwight D. Eisenhower. Statement by the President. The White House. July 29. 1958.
37. PL 85—766. Approved by the President. August 27. 1958.
38. Entire speech reprinted in the Final Report of the Special Committee on Space and Astronautics of the United States Senate. pursuant to S. Res. 256 of the 85th Congress. March 11. 1959. pp.58-62.
39. James R. Killian. Jr.. *Sputnik, Scientists, and Eisenhower* (Cambridge. MA: The MIT Press. 1977). p. 141.
40. See reference 31. Part 1. May 6. 1958. p. 8.

Appendix B

Additional Comments

by Eilene Galloway

1. *LBJ's Initial Reaction to Sputnik.*

Dr. Logsdon noted some discrepancies in accounts by participants. The discrepancy caused by George Reedy's questionable account of Senator Johnson's initial reaction to the orbiting of Sputnik can be cleared up by a factual citation of the Senator's actions immediately following the news on Friday, October 4, 1957 that the Soviet Union was first to launch a satellite into outer space.

LBJ was in Texas when the news broke and immediately he phoned the Chairman of the Senate Armed Services Committee, Senator Richard B. Russell. They realized that Sputnik demonstrated the capability of the Soviet Union for launching intercontinental ballistic missiles, instantly creating a problem for U.S. national defense. Senator Russell arranged for Senator Johnson, who was chairman of the Preparedness Investigating Subcommittee, to hold hearings on what became the "Inquiry Into Satellite and Missile Programs" (which began November 25, 1957). Senator Russell told LBJ that I could assist him with these hearings.

On Monday morning, October 7, Senator Russell phoned me and requested a report on "The Impact on the United States of the Soviet Union Being First to Launch a Satellite." Senator Johnson phoned me that morning and asked for my assistance, and I began on that day to concentrate on outer space problems. I was contacted because I was National Defense Analyst in the Congressional Research Service and for some time had been working for the Senate Armed Services Committee and some of its members, on organization of the Department of Defense, military man-power legislation, and questions for hearings with the Joint Chiefs of Staff. In the spring of 1957, I had written a report on "Guided Missiles in Foreign Countries" which was published by the House and Senate. Sputnik exploded on Capital Hill like a psychological bomb, arousing fears of orbiting weapons and consternation that the Soviet Union had taken the lead in rocketry. The general public reacted with alarm.

In this situation LBJ reacted swiftly and became the most energized leader I have ever beheld in galvanizing the Congress, the Pentagon, industry and the scientific community, to take decisive action to achieve U. S. preeminence in outer space.

How is it possible, therefore, to understand George Reedy's impression that "in the immediate aftermath, for about two weeks, I merely let the thing vegitate?" That he "sort of got the space thing on the back burner"; that "we [LBJ and Reedy] were down on the ranch pretty well isolated," and that LBJ "may have started out not so much opposed to, but with a feeling that this was nonsense." It was not until some days later that Reedy was briefed by Charles S. Brewton on the significance of Sputnik, and understood the implications of the situation. Then he wrote a positive memorandum to LBJ on October 17.

By October 17, I had been working for Senators Russell and Johnson for 10 days, and so had the Armed Services' staff and others in the Executive Branch.

My estimate of the situation is that LBJ's instinct was immediately to contact Senator Russell and military experts on the committee staff and in the Department of Defense. He had participated in the Committee's hearings on aspects of defense, including analyses of rockets. LBJ depended on Reedy for a variety of subjects—it was a time when civil rights had a priority—and although listed on the Preparedness Subcommittee staff, both Reedy and Gerry Siegel noted that for some time that subcommittee had been defunct—not so the permanent staff, however. My estimate is that George Reedy was not immediately aware of Sputnik's significance and because LBJ did not contact him, he assumed the Senator was not aroused by this event. Reedy was describing his own reactions and attributing them to the Senator. After Reedy returned to Washington, he was brought into the picture and had a briefing at the Pentagon and commented "that is where we *first* learned about Atlas and Polaris and all of those things," indicating that he first learned about some rockets.

I agree with Reedy that LBJ was not motivated by thoughts of running for President at that time—as he says, maybe earlier and later. LBJ was understandably anxious about his prospects for continuing health. I recall in San Antonio, he came to a flight of steps and ordinarily he would take them two at a time, but he looked slightly distressed and turned his steps to the elevator. However, I noticed that there were persons surrounding him who buzzed around because they were interested in his becoming president. But any historian who interprets LBJ's role in extending the U. S. into outer space as motivated by the presidency is cynical and misplacing his own reaction to the situation.

2. *Section 205 NASA's authority for international cooperation.*

I think the most significant action I ever took in my professional career concerned section 205 of the NASA Act on International Cooperation. Had the words added by Senator Green "by and with the advice and consent of the Senate" remained in the law without interpretation, NASA's program of international cooperation would have been restricted to formal treaty-type programs. The Senate Committee's purpose was to provide authority for international agreements in the broad range of projects essential for the development of space science and technology in a naturally international field. The U.S. has a variety of methods for accomplishing such objectives: treaties, executive agreements, agency-to-agency agreements, memoranda of understanding (MOUs) and letter agreements. It would have been counterproductive to restrict the means by which the agreed goal could be reached. The scope of NASA's international program was fortified by President Eisenhower's statement when he signed the bill that created NASA:

> The new act contains one provision that requires comment. Section 205 authorizes cooperation with other nations and groups of nations in work done pursuant to the act and in the peaceful application of the results of such work, pursuant to international agreements entered into by the President with the advice and consent of the Senate. I regard this section merely as recognizing that international treaties may be made in this field, and as not precluding, in appropriate cases, less formal arrangements for cooperation. To construe the section otherwise would raise substantial constitutional questions.

Later I prepared a Senate Document on "United States International Space Programs: Texts of Executive Agreements, Memoranda of Understanding, and Other International Arrangements, 1959–1965." (Senate document No. 44, 89th Congress, 1st session, Senate Committee on Aeronautical and Space Sciences. July 30, 1965. 575 P.) The introduction explains the different methods available for international cooperation, and under this authority NASA has agreements appropriate to the program, with over 100 countries.

3. *President Eisenhower and Senator Lyndon B. Johnson Cooperation on the Role of the United Nations in Outer Space.*

It seems to me that the historians and media have not paid sufficient attention to the dramatic event of the Republican President Eisenhower asking the Democratic leader of the U. S. Senate, Lyndon Johnson, to fly to the United Nations and get support for Eisenhower's proposal to create the Ad hoc Committee on the Peaceful Uses of Outer Space. Eisenhower sent a plane to Texas and LBJ flew with some staff to Laguardia in New York where he was met by our UN Ambassador Henry Cabot Lodge. LBJ addressed the UN on November 17, 1958 to express "the essential unity of the American people in their support of the goals of the resolution" proposed by President Eisenhower. The Committee was established and within a year became a permanent Committee with two subcommittees, Legal, and Scientific and Technical, growing from 24 to 61 members. This is the Committee that through the years has formulated five treaties on outer space.

This is an historic event of the President and Senate leader cooperating on a major foreign policy goal in spite of the fact that they were members of different political parties. As LBJ stated, "These are distinctions. They are not, on this resolution, differences."

4. *National Aeronautics and Space Council: Main Difference between Eisenhower's Proposed Legislation and the NASA Act as Passed by Congress.*

There was agreement on three main concepts in the proposal President Eisenhower sent to the Congress on April 2, 1958: to create a civilian space agency, to use the National Advisory Committee for Aeronautics (NACA) as the nucleus to expand into NASA, and that the Department of Defense should be responsible for space science and technology essential for its jurisdiction.

The difference that developed concerned the need for coordination in the Executive Branch. The Senate was not satisfied with the declaration of policy in the draft legislation concerning the relations between the new civilian agency and the Department of Defense. The draft proposed that NASA exercise control over aeronautical and space research except for those "peculiar to or primarily associated with weapons systems or military operating," and in such a case NASA "may act in cooperation with, or on behalf of DOD. Senator Russell rewrote the policy so that the lines of responsibility between NASA and DOD were clearer and gave the President responsibility for determining questions as to which such agency had responsibility.

I wrote the memorandum for Senator Johnson on the necessity for coordination by the National Aeronautics and Space Council, and the test is in the Final Report of the Senate Special Committee on Space and Astronautics, Senate report No. 100, 86th Congress, 1st session, March 11, 1959, pp. 3–12. I called it a board because they had been discussing the board of NACA, and this was changed from board to council during the conference committee meeting. I asked NASA to send the Senate committee a chart showing the areas of scientific cooperation between NASA and other Federal Activities, and this on page 11 of the Final Report. Although the agencies changed, nevertheless the concept remained that space activities would be of concern to more agencies than NASA and DOD. I understand that later, Dr. Glennan, administrator of NASA, wished to recall this chart but by that time I had already sent it to the printer.

5. *Some Miscellaneous Points.*

Lyndon Johnson asked me to write an analysis of how Congress should be organized to handled legislation on space activities as the subject cut across committee jurisdictions. I have an account of this in the paper I wrote on "The U.S. Congress and Outer Space: From Sputnik to the Shuttle" published in "Between Sputnik and the Shuttle: New Perspective on American Astronautics" edited by Frederick C. Durant, III. History series of the American Astronautical Society, Vol. 3. San Diego, California 1981 pp. 139–157. Illustrated.

This is important in indicating the spread of space science and technology in enabling agencies to improve functions they were already performing; and in illustrating the necessity for matching organizations in the Executive Branch with those in the Congress, both for authorizing and appropriating funds.

I got the word "unnecessary" in the NASA Act Sec. 102 (C) (8) at a staff meeting with Senator Symington. Usually persons come to the Hill and prove their projects is marvelous because it prevents overlapping and duplication, so I had at first a hard time getting "unnecessary" before "duplication," but they finally agreed that DOD would need some activities that were similar to the civilian and should be allowed.

Appendix C

Public Law 85-568
85th Congress, H. R. 12575
July 29, 1958

AN ACT

To provide for research into problems of flight within and outside the earth's atmosphere, and for other purposes.

Be it enacted by the Senate and House of Representatives of the United States of America in Congress assembled,

National
Aeronautics
and Space
Act of 1958.

TITLE I—SHORT TITLE, DECLARATION OF POLICY, AND DEFINITIONS

SHORT TITLE

SEC. 101. This Act may be cited as the "National Aeronautics and Space Act of 1958".

DECLARATION OF POLICY AND PURPOSE

SEC. 102. (a) The Congress hereby declares that it is the policy of the United States that activities in space should be devoted to peaceful purposes for the benefit of all mankind.

(b) The Congress declares that the general welfare and security of the United States require that adequate provision be made for aeronautical and space activities. The Congress further declares that such activities shall be the responsibility of, and shall be directed by, a civilian agency exercising control over aeronautical and space activities sponsored by the United States, except that activities peculiar to or primarily associated with the development of weapons systems, military operations, or the defense of the United States (including the research and development necessary to make effective provision for the defense of the United States) shall be the responsibility of, and shall be directed by, the Department of Defense; and that determination as to which such agency has responsibility for and direction of any such activity shall be made by the President in conformity with section 201 (e).

72 Stat. 425.
72 Stat. 427.

(c) The aeronautical and space activities of the United States shall be conducted so as to contribute materially to one or more of the following objectives:

(1) The expansion of human knowledge of phenomena in the atmosphere and space;

(2) The improvement of the usefulness, performance, speed, safety, and efficiency of aeronautical and space vehicles;

(3) The development and operation of vehicles capable of carrying instruments, equipment, supplies, and living organisms through space;

(4) The establishment of long-range studies of the potential benefits to be gained from, the opportunities for, and the problems involved in the utilization of aeronautical and space activities for peaceful and scientific purposes;

(5) The preservation of the role of the United States as a leader in aeronautical and space science and technology and in the application thereof to the conduct of peaceful activities within and outside the atmosphere;

(6) The making available to agencies directly concerned with national defense of discoveries that have military value or significance, and the furnishing by such agencies, to the civilian agency established to direct and control nonmilitary aeronautical and space activities, of information as to discoveries which have value or significance to that agency;

61

Pub. Law 85-568 -2- July 29, 1958

(7) Cooperation by the United States with other nations and groups of nations in work done pursuant to this Act and in the peaceful application of the results thereof; and

(8) The most effective utilization of the scientific and engineering resources of the United States, with close cooperation among all interested agencies of the United States in order to avoid unnecessary duplication of effort, facilities, and equipment.

(d) It is the purpose of this Act to carry out and effectuate the policies declared in subsections (a), (b), and (c).

DEFINITIONS

SEC. 103. As used in this Act—

(1) the term "aeronautical and space activities" means (A) research into, and the solution of, problems of flight within and outside the earth's atmosphere, (B) the development, construction, testing, and operation for research purposes of aeronautical and space vehicles, and (C) such other activities as may be required for the exploration of space; and

(2) the term "aeronautical and space vehicles" means aircraft, missiles, satellites, and other space vehicles, manned and unmanned, together with related equipment, devices, components, and parts.

TITLE II—COORDINATION OF AERONAUTICAL AND SPACE ACTIVITIES

NATIONAL AERONAUTICS AND SPACE COUNCIL

Establishment. SEC. 201. (a) There is hereby established the National Aeronautics and Space Council (hereinafter called the "Council") which shall be composed of—

(1) the President (who shall preside over meetings of the Council);

72 Stat. 427.
72 Stat. 428.

(2) the Secretary of State;

(3) the Secretary of Defense;

(4) the Administrator of the National Aeronautics and Space Administration;

(5) the Chairman of the Atomic Energy Commission;

(6) not more than one additional member appointed by the President from the departments and agencies of the Federal Government; and

(7) not more than three other members appointed by the President, solely on the basis of established records of distinguished achievement, from among individuals in private life who are eminent in science, engineering, technology, education, administration, or public affairs.

Alternate. (b) Each member of the Council from a department or agency of the Federal Government may designate another officer of his department or agency to serve on the Council as his alternate in his unavoidable absence.

(c) Each member of the Council appointed or designated under paragraphs (6) and (7) of subsection (a), and each alternate member designated under subsection (b), shall be appointed or designated to serve as such by and with the advice and consent of the Senate, unless at the time of such appointment or designation he holds an office in the Federal Government to which he was appointed by and with the advice and consent of the Senate.

July 29, 1958   -3-   Pub. Law 85-568

(d) It shall be the function of the Council to advise the President with respect to the performance of the duties prescribed in subsection (e) of this section.

(e) In conformity with the provisions of section 102 of this Act, it shall be the duty of the President to—   *Duties of President.*

    (1) survey all significant aeronautical and space activities, including the policies, plans, programs, and accomplishments of all agencies of the United States engaged in such activities;

    (2) develop a comprehensive program of aeronautical and space activities to be conducted by agencies of the United States;

    (3) designate and fix responsibility for the direction of major aeronautical and space activities;

    (4) provide for effective cooperation between the National Aeronautics and Space Administration and the Department of Defense in all such activities, and specify which of such activities may be carried on concurrently by both such agencies notwithstanding the assignment of primary responsibility therefor to one or the other of such agencies; and

    (5) resolve differences arising among departments and agencies of the United States with respect to aeronautical and space activities under this Act, including differences as to whether a particular project is an aeronautical and space activity.

(f) The Council may employ a staff to be headed by a civilian executive secretary who shall be appointed by the President by and with the advice and consent of the Senate and shall receive compensation at the rate of $20,000 a year. The executive secretary, subject to the direction of the Council, is authorized to appoint and fix the compensation of such personnel, including not more than three persons who may be appointed without regard to the civil service laws or the Classification Act of 1949 and compensated at the rate of not more than $19,000 a year, as may be necessary to perform such duties as may be prescribed by the Council in connection with the performance of its functions. Each appointment under this subsection shall be subject to the same security requirements as those established for personnel of the National Aeronautics and Space Administration appointed under section 203 (b) (2) of this Act.   *Employees. Compensation.*   *63 Stat. 954. 5 USC 1071 note.*   *Security check.*

(g) Members of the Council appointed from private life under subsection (a) (7) may be compensated at a rate not to exceed $100 per diem, and may be paid travel expenses and per diem in lieu of subsistence in accordance with the provisions of section 5 of the Administrative Expenses Act of 1946 (5 U. S. C. 73b-2) relating to persons serving without compensation.   *Per diem.*   *72 Stat. 428. 72 Stat. 429.*   *69 Stat. 394.*

NATIONAL AERONAUTICS AND SPACE ADMINISTRATION

SEC. 202. (a) There is hereby established the National Aeronautics and Space Administration (hereinafter called the "Administration"). The Administration shall be headed by an Administrator, who shall be appointed from civilian life by the President by and with the advice and consent of the Senate, and shall receive compensation at the rate of $22,500 per annum. Under the supervision and direction of the President, the Administrator shall be responsible for the exercise of all powers and the discharge of all duties of the Administration, and shall have authority and control over all personnel and activities thereof.   *Administrator.*

(b) There shall be in the Administration a Deputy Administrator, who shall be appointed from civilian life by the President by and with the advice and consent of the Senate, shall receive compensation at the rate of $21,500 per annum, and shall perform such duties and exercise   *Deputy Administrator.*

Pub. Law 85-568   -4-   July 29, 1958

such powers as the Administrator may prescribe. The Deputy Administrator shall act for, and exercise the powers of, the Administrator during his absence or disability.

Restriction. (c) The Administrator and the Deputy Administrator shall not engage in any other business, vocation, or employment while serving as such.

FUNCTIONS OF THE ADMINISTRATION

SEC. 203. (a) The Administration, in order to carry out the purpose of this Act, shall—

(1) plan, direct, and conduct aeronautical and space activities;

(2) arrange for participation by the scientific community in planning scientific measurements and observations to be made through use of aeronautical and space vehicles, and conduct or arrange for the conduct of such measurements and observations; and

(3) provide for the widest practicable and appropriate dissemination of information concerning its activities and the results thereof.

(b) In the performance of its functions the Administration is authorized—

Rules and regulations. (1) to make, promulgate, issue, rescind, and amend rules and regulations governing the manner of its operations and the exercise of the powers vested in it by law;

Employees. (2) to appoint and fix the compensation of such officers and employees as may be necessary to carry out such functions. Such officers and employees shall be appointed in accordance with the civil-service laws and their compensation fixed in accordance with the Classification Act of 1949, except that (A) to the extent the Administrator deems such action necessary to the discharge of his responsibilities, he may appoint and fix the compensation (up to a limit of $19,000 a year, or up to a limit of $21,000 a year for a maximum of ten positions) of not more than two hundred and sixty of the scientific, engineering, and administrative personnel of the Administration without regard to such laws, and (B) to the extent the Administrator deems such action necessary to recruit specially qualified scientific and engineering talent, he may establish the entrance grade for scientific and engineering personnel without previous service in the Federal Government at a level up to two grades higher than the grade provided for such personnel under the General Schedule established by the Classification Act of 1949, and fix their compensation accordingly;

63 Stat. 954, 5 USC 1071 note.

72 Stat. 429, 72 Stat. 430.

Acquisition of property. (3) to acquire (by purchase, lease, condemnation, or otherwise), construct, improve, repair, operate, and maintain laboratories, research and testing sites and facilities, aeronautical and space vehicles, quarters and related accommodations for employees and dependents of employees of the Administration, and such other real and personal property (including patents), or any interest therein, as the Administration deems necessary within and outside the continental United States; to lease to others such real and personal property; to sell and otherwise dispose of real and personal property (including patents and rights thereunder) in accordance with the provisions of the Federal Property and Administrative Services Act of 1949, as amended (40 U. S. C. 471 et seq.); and to provide by contract or otherwise for cafeterias and other necessary facilities for the welfare of employees of the Administration at its installations and purchase and maintain equipment therefor;

63 Stat. 377.

July 29, 1958   -5-   Pub. Law 85-568

(4) to accept unconditional gifts or donations of services, **Gifts.** money, or property, real, personal, or mixed, tangible or intangible;

(5) without regard to section 3648 of the Revised Statutes, as **Contracts,** amended (31 U. S. C. 529), to enter into and perform such con- **etc.** tracts, leases, cooperative agreements, or other transactions as may **60 Stat. 809.** be necessary in the conduct of its work and on such terms as it may deem appropriate, with any agency or instrumentality of the United States, or with any State, Territory, or possession, or with any political subdivision thereof, or with any person, firm, association, corporation, or educational institution. To the maximum extent practicable and consistent with the accomplishment of the purpose of this Act, such contracts, leases, agreements, and other transactions shall be allocated by the Administrator in a manner which will enable small business concerns to participate equitably and proportionately in the conduct of the work of the Administration;

(6) to use, with their consent, the services, equipment, personnel, **Agency** and facilities of Federal and other agencies with or without reim- **cooperation.** bursement, and on a similar basis to cooperate with other public and private agencies and instrumentalities in the use of services, equipment, and facilities. Each department and agency of the Federal Government shall cooperate fully with the Administration in making its services, equipment, personnel, and facilities available to the Administration, and any such department or agency is authorized, notwithstanding any other provision of law, to transfer to or to receive from the Administration, without reimbursement, aeronautical and space vehicles, and supplies and equipment other than administrative supplies or equipment;

(7) to appoint such advisory committees as may be appropriate **Advisory** for purposes of consultation and advice to the Administration in **committees.** the performance of its functions;

(8) to establish within the Administration such offices and pro- **Coordination.** cedures as may be appropriate to provide for the greatest possible coordination of its activities under this Act with related scientific and other activities being carried on by other public and private **72 Stat. 430.** agencies and organizations; **72 Stat. 431.**

(9) to obtain services as authorized by section 15 of the Act of August 2, 1946 (5 U. S. C. 55a), at rates not to exceed $100 per **60 Stat. 810.** diem for individuals;

(10) when determined by the Administrator to be necessary, **Employment.** and subject to such security investigations as he may determine **Aliens.** to be appropriate, to employ aliens without regard to statutory provisions prohibiting payment of compensation to aliens;

(11) to employ retired commissioned officers of the armed **Retired** forces of the United States and compensate them at the rate estab- **officers.** lished for the positions occupied by them within the Administration, subject only to the limitations in pay set forth in section 212 of the Act of June 30, 1932, as amended (5 U. S. C. 59a); **68 Stat. 18.**

(12) with the approval of the President, to enter into coopera- **Agreements.** tive agreements under which members of the Army, Navy, Air Force, and Marine Corps may be detailed by the appropriate Secretary for services in the performance of functions under this Act to the same extent as that to which they might be lawfully assigned in the Department of Defense; and

(13) (A) to consider, ascertain, adjust, determine, settle, and **Claims.** pay, on behalf of the United States, in full satisfaction thereof, any claim for $5,000 or less against the United States for bodily injury, death, or damage to or loss of real or personal property

Pub. Law 85-568   -6-   July 29, 1958

resulting from the conduct of the Administration's functions as specified in subsection (a) of this section, where such claim is presented to the Administration in writing within two years after the accident or incident out of which the claim arises; and

Report to
Congress.

(B) if the Administration considers that a claim in excess of $5,000 is meritorious and would otherwise be covered by this paragraph, to report the facts and circumstances thereof to the Congress for its consideration.

CIVILIAN-MILITARY LIAISON COMMITTEE

SEC. 204. (a) There shall be a Civilian-Military Liaison Committee consisting of—

(1) a Chairman, who shall be the head thereof and who shall be appointed by the President, shall serve at the pleasure of the President, and shall receive compensation (in the manner provided in subsection (d)) at the rate of $20,000 per annum;

(2) one or more representatives from the Department of Defense, and one or more representatives from each of the Departments of the Army, Navy, and Air Force, to be assigned by the Secretary of Defense to serve on the Committee without additional compensation; and

(3) representatives from the Administration, to be assigned by the Administrator to serve on the Committee without additional compensation, equal in number to the number of representatives assigned to serve on the Committee under paragraph (2).

(b) The Administration and the Department of Defense, through the Liaison Committee, shall advise and consult with each other on all matters within their respective jurisdictions relating to aeronautical and space activities and shall keep each other fully and currently informed with respect to such activities.

(c) If the Secretary of Defense concludes that any request, action, proposed action, or failure to act on the part of the Administrator is adverse to the responsibilities of the Department of Defense, or the Administrator concludes that any request, action, proposed action, or failure to act on the part of the Department of Defense is adverse to the responsibilities of the Administration, and the Administrator and the Secretary of Defense are unable to reach an agreement with respect thereto, either the Administrator or the Secretary of Defense may refer the matter to the President for his decision (which shall be final) as provided in section 201 (e).

72 Stat. 431.
72 Stat. 432.

Chairman.

(d) Notwithstanding the provisions of any other law, any active or retired officer of the Army, Navy, or Air Force may serve as Chairman of the Liaison Committee without prejudice to his active or retired status as such officer. The compensation received by any such officer for his service as Chairman of the Liaison Committee shall be equal to the amount (if any) by which the compensation fixed by subsection (a) (1) for such Chairman exceeds his pay and allowances (including special and incentive pays) as an active officer, or his retired pay.

INTERNATIONAL COOPERATION

SEC. 205. The Administration, under the foreign policy guidance of the President, may engage in a program of international cooperation in work done pursuant to this Act, and in the peaceful application of the results thereof, pursuant to agreements made by the President with the advice and consent of the Senate.

July 29, 1958   -7-   Pub. Law 85-568

REPORTS TO THE CONGRESS

SEC. 206. (a) The Administration shall submit to the President for transmittal to the Congress, semiannually and at such other times as it deems desirable, a report of its activities and accomplishments.

(b) The President shall transmit to the Congress in January of each year a report, which shall include (1) a comprehensive description of the programed activities and the accomplishments of all agencies of the United States in the field of aeronautics and space activities during the preceding calendar year, and (2) an evaluation of such activities and accomplishments in terms of the attainment of, or the failure to attain, the objectives described in section 102 (c) of this Act.

(c) Any report made under this section shall contain such recommendations for additional legislation as the Administrator or the President may consider necessary or desirable for the attainment of the objectives described in section 102 (c) of this Act.

(d) No information which has been classified for reasons of national security shall be included in any report made under this section, unless such information has been declassified by, or pursuant to authorization given by, the President.

TITLE III—MISCELLANEOUS

NATIONAL ADVISORY COMMITTEE FOR AERONAUTICS

SEC. 301. (a) The National Advisory Committee for Aeronautics, on the effective date of this section, shall cease to exist. On such date all functions, powers, duties, and obligations, and all real and personal property, personnel (other than members of the Committee), funds, and records of that organization, shall be transferred to the Administration.
Termination. Transfer of functions.

(b) Section 2302 of title 10 of the United States Code is amended by striking out "or the Executive Secretary of the National Advisory Committee for Aeronautics." and inserting in lieu thereof "or the Administrator of the National Aeronautics and Space Administration."; and section 2303 of such title 10 is amended by striking out "The National Advisory Committee for Aeronautics." and inserting in lieu thereof "The National Aeronautics and Space Administration."
Definitions. 70A Stat. 127.

(c) The first section of the Act of August 26, 1950 (5 U. S. C. 22-1), is amended by striking out "the Director, National Advisory Committee for Aeronautics" and inserting in lieu thereof "the Administrator of the National Aeronautics and Space Administration", and by striking out "or National Advisory Committee for Aeronautics" and inserting in lieu thereof "or National Aeronautics and Space Administration".
64 Stat. 476. 72 Stat. 432. 72 Stat. 433.

(d) The Unitary Wind Tunnel Plan Act of 1949 (50 U. S. C. 511-515) is amended (1) by striking out "The National Advisory Committee for Aeronautics (hereinafter referred to as the 'Committee')" and inserting in lieu thereof "The Administrator of the National Aeronautics and Space Administration (hereinafter referred to as the 'Administrator')"; (2) by striking out "Committee" or "Committee's" wherever they appear and inserting in lieu thereof "Administrator" and "Administrator's", respectively; and (3) by striking out "its" wherever it appears and inserting in lieu thereof "his".
63 Stat. 936.

(e) This section shall take effect ninety days after the date of the enactment of this Act, or on any earlier date on which the Administrator shall determine, and announce by proclamation published in the Federal Register, that the Administration has been organized and is prepared to discharge the duties and exercise the powers conferred upon it by this Act.
Effective date.
Publication in F.R.

Pub. Law 85-568   -8-   July 29, 1958

TRANSFER OF RELATED FUNCTIONS

SEC. 302. (a) Subject to the provisions of this section, the President, for a period of four years after the date of enactment of this Act, may transfer to the Administration any functions (including powers, duties, activities, facilities, and parts of functions) of any other department or agency of the United States, or of any officer or organizational entity thereof, which relate primarily to the functions, powers, and duties of the Administration as prescribed by section 203 of this Act. In connection with any such transfer, the President may, under this section or other applicable authority, provide for appropriate transfers of records, property, civilian personnel, and funds.

Reports to Congress.

(b) Whenever any such transfer is made before January 1, 1959, the President shall transmit to the Speaker of the House of Representatives and the President pro tempore of the Senate a full and complete report concerning the nature and effect of such transfer.

(c) After December 31, 1958, no transfer shall be made under this section until (1) a full and complete report concerning the nature and effect of such proposed transfer has been transmitted by the President to the Congress, and (2) the first period of sixty calendar days of regular session of the Congress following the date of receipt of such report by the Congress has expired without the adoption by the Congress of a concurrent resolution stating that the Congress does not favor such transfer.

ACCESS TO INFORMATION

SEC. 303. Information obtained or developed by the Administrator in the performance of his functions under this Act shall be made available for public inspection, except (A) information authorized or required by Federal statute to be withheld, and (B) information classified to protect the national security: *Provided*, That nothing in this Act shall authorize the withholding of information by the Administrator from the duly authorized committees of the Congress.

SECURITY

Requirements.

72 Stat. 433.
72 Stat. 434.

SEC. 304. (a) The Administrator shall establish such security requirements, restrictions, and safeguards as he deems necessary in the interest of the national security. The Administrator may arrange with the Civil Service Commission for the conduct of such security or other personnel investigations of the Administration's officers, employees, and consultants, and its contractors and subcontractors and their officers and employees, actual or prospective, as he deems appropriate; and if any such investigation develops any data reflecting that the individual who is the subject thereof is of questionable loyalty the matter shall be referred to the Federal Bureau of Investigation for the conduct of a full field investigation, the results of which shall be furnished to the Administrator.

Referral to F.B.I.

Access to AEC restricted data.

68 Stat. 942.

(b) The Atomic Energy Commission may authorize any of its employees, or employees of any contractor, prospective contractor, licensee, or prospective licensee of the Atomic Energy Commission or any other person authorized to have access to Restricted Data by the Atomic Energy Commission under subsection 145 b. of the Atomic Energy Act of 1954 (42 U. S. C. 2165 (b)), to permit any member, officer, or employee of the Council, or the Administrator, or any officer, employee, member of an advisory committee, contractor, subcontractor, or officer or employee of a contractor or subcontractor of the Administration, to have access to Restricted Data relating to aeronautical and space activities which is required in the performance of his duties and so certified by the Council or the Administrator, as the case may be,

July 29, 1958   -9-   Pub. Law 85-568

but only if (1) the Council or Administrator or designee thereof has determined, in accordance with the established personnel security procedures and standards of the Council or Administration, that permitting such individual to have access to such Restricted Data will not endanger the common defense and security, and (2) the Council or Administrator or designee thereof finds that the established personnel and other security procedures and standards of the Council or Administration are adequate and in reasonable conformity to the standards established by the Atomic Energy Commission under section 145 of the Atomic Energy Act of 1954 (42 U. S. C. 2165). Any individual granted access to such Restricted Data pursuant to this subsection may exchange such Data with any individual who (A) is an officer or employee of the Department of Defense, or any department or agency thereof, or a member of the armed forces, or a contractor or subcontractor of any such department, agency, or armed force, or an officer or employee of any such contractor or subcontractor, and (B) has been authorized to have access to Restricted Data under the provisions of section 143 of the Atomic Energy Act of 1954 (42 U. S. C. 2163).

68 Stat. 942.

(c) Chapter 37 of title 18 of the United States Code (entitled Espionage and Censorship) is amended by—

(1) adding at the end thereof the following new section:

Espionage and Censorship. 62 Stat. 736–738;65 Stat. 719. 18 USC 791–798. Violation.

"§ 799. Violation of regulations of National Aeronautics and Space Administration

"Whoever willfully shall violate, attempt to violate, or conspire to violate any regulation or order promulgated by the Administrator of the National Aeronautics and Space Administration for the protection or security of any laboratory, station, base or other facility, or part thereof, or any aircraft, missile, spacecraft, or similar vehicle, or part thereof, or other property or equipment in the custody of the Administration, or any real or personal property or equipment in the custody of any contractor under any contract with the Administration or any subcontractor of any such contractor, shall be fined not more than $5,000, or imprisoned not more than one year, or both."

Penalty.

(2) adding at the end of the sectional analysis thereof the following new item:

"799. Violation of regulations of National Aeronautics and Space Administration."

72 Stat. 434. 72 Stat. 435. Protection of U.S. officers and employees. 62 Stat. 756.

(d) Section 1114 of title 18 of the United States Code is amended by inserting immediately before "while engaged in the performance of his official duties" the following: "or any officer or employee of the National Aeronautics and Space Administration directed to guard and protect property of the United States under the administration and control of the National Aeronautics and Space Administration.".

(e) The Administrator may direct such of the officers and employees of the Administration as he deems necessary in the public interest to carry firearms while in the conduct of their official duties. The Administrator may also authorize such of those employees of the contractors and subcontractors of the Administration engaged in the protection of property owned by the United States and located at facilities owned by or contracted to the United States as he deems necessary in the public interest, to carry firearms while in the conduct of their official duties.

Permission to use firearms.

PROPERTY RIGHTS IN INVENTIONS

SEC. 305. (a) Whenever any invention is made in the performance of any work under any contract of the Administration, and the Administrator determines that—

(1) the person who made the invention was employed or assigned to perform research, development, or exploration work and the invention is related to the work he was employed or

Pub. Law 85-568   -10-   July 29, 1958

assigned to perform, or that it was within the scope of his employment duties, whether or not it was made during working hours,
or with a contribution by the Government of the use of Government facilities, equipment, materials, allocated funds, information proprietary to the Government, or services of Government
employees during working hours; or

(2) the person who made the invention was not employed or
assigned to perform research, development, or exploration work,
but the invention is nevertheless related to the contract, or to the
work or duties he was employed or assigned to perform, and was
made during working hours, or with a contribution from the
Government of the sort referred to in clause (1),

such invention shall be the exclusive property of the United States,
and if such invention is patentable a patent therefor shall be issued
to the United States upon application made by the Administrator,
unless the Administrator waives all or any part of the rights of the
United States to such invention in conformity with the provisions of
subsection (f) of this section.

Contract
provision.

(b) Each contract entered into by the Administrator with any
party for the performance of any work shall contain effective provisions under which such party shall furnish promptly to the Administrator a written report containing full and complete technical
information concerning any invention, discovery, improvement, or
innovation which may be made in the performance of any such work.

Patent
application.

(c) No patent may be issued to any applicant other than the Administrator for any invention which appears to the Commissioner of Patents to have significant utility in the conduct of aeronautical and space
activities unless the applicant files with the Commissioner, with the
application or within thirty days after request therefor by the Commissioner, a written statement executed under oath setting forth the
full facts concerning the circumstances under which such invention was
made and stating the relationship (if any) of such invention to the
performance of any work under any contract of the Administration.
Copies of each such statement and the application to which it relates
shall be transmitted forthwith by the Commissioner to the Administrator.

72 Stat. 435.
72 Stat. 436.

Board of Patent
Interferences.

(d) Upon any application as to which any such statement has been
transmitted to the Administrator, the Commissioner may, if the invention is patentable, issue a patent to the applicant unless the Administrator, within ninety days after receipt of such application and statement, requests that such patent be issued to him on behalf of the United
States. If, within such time, the Administrator files such a request
with the Commissioner, the Commissioner shall transmit notice thereof
to the applicant, and shall issue such patent to the Administrator
unless the applicant within thirty days after receipt of such notice
requests a hearing before a Board of Patent Interferences on the question whether the Administrator is entitled under this section to receive
such patent. The Board may hear and determine, in accordance with
rules and procedures established for interference cases, the question
so presented, and its determination shall be subject to appeal by the
applicant or by the Administrator to the Court of Customs and Patent
Appeals in accordance with procedures governing appeals from decisions of the Board of Patent Interferences in other proceedings.

(e) Whenever any patent has been issued to any applicant in conformity with subsection (d), and the Administrator thereafter has
reason to believe that the statement filed by the applicant in connection therewith contained any false representation of any material
fact, the Administrator within five years after the date of issuance
of such patent may file with the Commissioner a request for the trans-

July 29, 1958   -11-   Pub. Law 85-568

fer to the Administrator of title to such patent on the records of the Commissioner. Notice of any such request shall be transmitted by the Commissioner to the owner of record of such patent, and title to such patent shall be so transferred to the Administrator unless within thirty days after receipt of such notice such owner of record requests a hearing before a Board of Patent Interferences on the question whether any such false representation was contained in such statement. Such question shall be heard and determined, and determination thereof shall be subject to review, in the manner prescribed by subsection (d) for questions arising thereunder. No request made by the Administrator under this subsection for the transfer of title to any patent, and no prosecution for the violation of any criminal statute, shall be barred by any failure of the Administrator to make a request under subsection (d) for the issuance of such patent to him, or by any notice previously given by the Administrator stating that he had no objection to the issuance of such patent to the applicant therefor.

(f) Under such regulations in conformity with this subsection as the Administrator shall prescribe, he may waive all or any part of the rights of the United States under this section with respect to any invention or class of inventions made or which may be made by any person or class of persons in the performance of any work required by any contract of the Administration if the Administrator determines that the interests of the United States will be served thereby. Any such waiver may be made upon such terms and under such conditions as the Administrator shall determine to be required for the protection of the interests of the United States. Each such waiver made with respect to any invention shall be subject to the reservation by the Administrator of an irrevocable, nonexclusive, nontransferrable, royalty-free license for the practice of such invention throughout the world by or on behalf of the United States or any foreign government pursuant to any treaty or agreement with the United States. Each proposal for any waiver under this subsection shall be referred to an Inventions and Contributions Board which shall be established by the Administrator within the Administration. Such Board shall accord to each interested party an opportunity for hearing, and shall transmit to the Administrator its findings of fact with respect to such proposal and its recommendations for action to be taken with respect thereto. *(Waiver.)* *(Inventions and Contributions Board.)*

(g) The Administrator shall determine, and promulgate regulations specifying, the terms and conditions upon which licenses will be granted by the Administration for the practice by any person (other than an agency of the United States) of any invention for which the Administrator holds a patent on behalf of the United States. *(License regulations.)* *(72 Stat. 436.)* *(72 Stat. 437.)*

(h) The Administrator is authorized to take all suitable and necessary steps to protect any invention or discovery to which he has title, and to require that contractors or persons who retain title to inventions or discoveries under this section protect the inventions or discoveries to which the Administration has or may acquire a license of use. *(Protection of title.)*

(i) The Administration shall be considered a defense agency of the United States for the purpose of chapter 17 of title 35 of the United States Code. *(Defense agency. 66 Stat. 805-808.)*

(j) As used in this section— *(Definitions.)*

    (1) the term "person" means any individual, partnership, corporation, association, institution, or other entity;

    (2) the term "contract" means any actual or proposed contract, agreement, understanding, or other arrangement, and includes any assignment, substitution of parties, or subcontract executed or entered into thereunder; and

(3) the term "made", when used in relation to any invention, means the conception or first actual reduction to practice of such invention.

CONTRIBUTIONS AWARDS

SEC. 306. (a) Subject to the provisions of this section, the Administrator is authorized, upon his own initiative or upon application of any person, to make a monetary award, in such amount and upon such terms as he shall determine to be warranted, to any person (as defined by section 305) for any scientific or technical contribution to the Administration which is determined by the Administrator to have significant value in the conduct of aeronautical and space activities. Each application made for any such award shall be referred to the Inventions and Contributions Board established under section 305 of this Act. Such Board shall accord to each such applicant an opportunity for hearing upon such application, and shall transmit to the Administrator its recommendation as to the terms of the award, if any, to be made to such applicant for such contribution. In determining the terms and conditions of any award the Administrator shall take into account—

(1) the value of the contribution to the United States;

(2) the aggregate amount of any sums which have been expended by the applicant for the development of such contribution;

(3) the amount of any compensation (other than salary received for services rendered as an officer or employee of the Government) previously received by the applicant for or on account of the use of such contribution by the United States; and

(4) such other factors as the Administrator shall determine to be material.

(b) If more than one applicant under subsection (a) claims an interest in the same contribution, the Administrator shall ascertain and determine the respective interests of such applicants, and shall apportion any award to be made with respect to such contribution among such applicants in such proportions as he shall determine to be equitable. No award may be made under subsection (a) with respect to any contribution—

(1) unless the applicant surrenders, by such means as the Administrator shall determine to be effective, all claims which such applicant may have to receive any compensation (other than the award made under this section) for the use of such contribution or any element thereof at any time by or on behalf of the United States, or by or on behalf of any foreign government pursuant to any treaty or agreement with the United States, within the United States or at any other place;

(2) in any amount exceeding $100,000, unless the Administrator has transmitted to the appropriate committees of the Congress a full and complete report concerning the amount and terms of, and the basis for, such proposed award, and thirty calendar days of regular session of the Congress have expired after receipt of such report by such committees.

72 Stat. 437.
72 Stat. 438.

July 29, 1958   -13-   Pub. Law 85-568
                                      72 Stat. 438,

APPROPRIATIONS

SEC. 307. (a) There are hereby authorized to be appropriated such sums as may be necessary to carry out this Act, except that nothing in this Act shall authorize the appropriation of any amount for (1) the acquisition or condemnation of any real property, or (2) any other item of a capital nature (such as plant or facility acquisition, construction, or expansion) which exceeds $250,000. Sums appropriated pursuant to this subsection for the construction of facilities, or for research and development activities, shall remain available until expended.

(b) Any funds appropriated for the construction of facilities may be used for emergency repairs of existing facilities when such existing facilities are made inoperative by major breakdown, accident, or other circumstances and such repairs are deemed by the Administrator to be of greater urgency than the construction of new facilities.

Approved July 29, 1958.

Index

*U.S. Government Printing Office: 1998 — 433-387/96501

www.ingramcontent.com/pod-product-compliance
Lightning Source LLC
Chambersburg PA
CBHW081237090426

42738CB00016B/3333